POETRY COMPETITION
FOR 11-18 YEAR-OLDS

POP!
The Power Of Poetry

Scotland Vol I
Edited by Steve Twelvetree

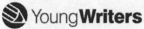 Young**Writers**

First published in Great Britain in 2006 by:
Young Writers
Remus House
Coltsfoot Drive
Peterborough
PE2 9JX
Telephone: 01733 890066
Website: www.youngwriters.co.uk

SB ISBN 1 84602 396 3

Foreword

This year, the Young Writers' *POP! - The Power Of Poetry* competition proudly presents a showcase of the best poetic talent selected from thousands of up-and-coming writers nationwide.

Young Writers was established in 1991 to promote the reading and writing of poetry within schools and to the young of today. Our books nurture and inspire confidence in the ability of young writers and provide a snapshot of poems written in schools and at home by budding poets of the future.

The thought, effort, imagination and hard work put into each poem impressed us all and the task of selecting poems was a difficult but nevertheless enjoyable experience.

We hope you are as pleased as we are with the final selection and that you and your family continue to be entertained with *POP! Scotland Vol I* for many years to come.

Contents

Amanda Jamieson (13)   49
Aisling Gilbert (11)   50
Chantal Walker (12)   50
Fraser Coyle (13)   51
Lorna McIntyre (12)   51
Chloë Aitchison (13)   51
Connor Fulton (12)   52
Ben Gardiner (12)   52
David Guthrie (13)   53
Ainsley Boyle (13)   53
Jennifer Cooney (13)   54
Scott Gemmell (12)   54
Iain McCabe (12)   54
Shannon Coubrough (11)   55
Kirsty Crawford (12)   55
Craig Baxter (12)   55
Sarah Tweedly (12)   56
Fraser Stewart (12)   56
Michael Collins (12)   56
Fiona Gemmell (12)   57
Evelyn Matthew (11)   58
Graham Gay (12)   59
Emma Renton (11)   59
Adam McDermott (12)   60

Grove Academy, Broughty Ferry
Jenny Ferguson (14)   60
Alison Wong (14)   61
Louise Hurrell (13)   62
Caitlin McLeish (14)   63
Joanne Findlay (14)   64

High School of Dundee, Dundee
Alex Montgomery (13)   64
Rachael Spink (13)   65
Jamie Johnston (13)   65
Kirsty McEwan (13)   66
Heather Gray (13)   67
Charlotte Keatch (12)   68
Vanita Nathwani (13)   69
Lynsey Brown (12)   70

Anna Mackenzie (11)	71
Kirsty Mitchell (12)	72
Tristan Leicester (12)	73
Rebecca Reid (11)	74
Siobhan Chien (11)	75
Alistair Lynch (12)	76
Freya Drummond (11)	77
Harry Ogilvie (12)	78
Madeleine Adamson (12)	79
David Bruce (12)	80
Suzie Brown (11)	81
Alistair Bell (13)	82
Ewain Black (14)	83
Kirsty Kilpatrick (13)	84

Invergordon Academy, Invergordon

Rachel Benson (13)	84
Donna Dunn (13)	85
Tara Docherty (16)	85
Tanya Calder (12)	86
Jordan Mitchell (16)	86
Emily Goodwin (13)	87
Daniel Hogarth (16)	87
Thomas Baird (13)	88
Kerry Armstrong (12)	88
Sean Sutherland (13)	89
Sarah Sinclair (13)	89
Wendy Brown (12)	90
Rachael Bews (13)	91
Mairi M MacLeod (13)	92
Amy Bremner (13)	93
Liam Irvine (13)	94
Rachel Michael (13)	95
Dean Thomson (13)	96
Alasdair Turner (13)	97
Robert Michael (13)	98
Carly Yeaman (13)	99
Lynn Semple (12)	100
Jasmin Ross (13)	101
Erin Robson (13)	102

Kelso High School, Kelso

Diane Whittle (15)	102
Stephanie Cockburn (14)	103
Carrie Jardine (15)	103
Craig Watson (13)	104
Jamie Mitchell (15)	104
Phillip Hume (15)	105
Paul Simpson (15)	105
Kerry Bell (14)	106
Vicki Freshwater (14)	107
Steven Robson (14)	108
Amanda Charters (15)	108
Katie Pettigrew (12)	109
Grant Charters (12)	109
Georgina Woodhead (14)	110
Kayleigh Beveridge (14)	111
Bryony Nisbet (14)	112
Robyn Hall (14)	113
Rachel Waters (15)	114
Claire Page (15)	114
Steven Jeffrey (15)	115
Calum Bruce (15)	115
Rhona Anderson (15)	116
Michelle Condy-Smith (15)	117
Andrew Hogarth (15)	118
Megan Wilde (15)	118
Laura Mulvie (12)	119
Sarah Watson (15)	119
Katie Holmes-Smith (15)	120
Sarah Strathdee (13)	120
Jenna Simpson (13)	121
Rachel Butler (13)	121
Lesley Chaman (13)	122
David Sanderson (13)	123
Jamie Noble (13)	123
Ashley Fairbairn (14)	124
Tanyta Johnston (13)	124
Shaun McNulty (14)	125
Callum Patterson (12)	125
Hayley Ker (14)	126
Jamie Norman (13)	126

Neil McGuigan (14)	127
Lisa Jeffrey (12)	127
Scott Morris (13)	128
Michael Portsmouth (15)	129
Carmen Falla (13)	129
Emma Thoms (13)	130
Yasmin Boni (14)	131
Robin Chapman (15)	132
Richard Marshall (13)	132
Stuart Lowrie (14)	133
Anna Ramsay (12)	133
Jamie Heppell (15)	134
Alexis Collins (12)	135
Paul Burke (14)	136
Thomas Gascoigne (15)	136
Rachael Sudlow (14)	137
Oliver Cunningham (15)	137
Rebecca Corbett (12)	138
Carol-Ann Noble (13)	138
Dan Barnes (12)	139
Emma Bain (15)	140
Laura Gibson (13)	140
John Scott (12)	141
Matthew Fenwick (12)	142
Andrew Dodds (13)	142
Murray Hastie (13)	143
Natasha Hewson (13)	143
Lucy Harding (12)	144
Jenny Brunton (12)	145
Stuart Skeldon (11)	146
Scott Tonner (12)	147
James Stewart (12)	148
Jason Scott (11)	148
Kevin Trotter (12)	149
Louise Cowan (12)	149
Kieran Flannigan (12)	150
Stephanie Rae (12)	151
Carly Green (11)	152
George Knox (13)	153
Gillian Forsyth (12)	154
Fraser McFarlane (12)	154
Michelle Ewart (12)	155

Allie Young (14)   181
Andrew Thomson (12)   182
Terri Wight (12)   183
Ian Henderson (16)   184
Fiona Black (12)   184
Ashley Gibson (16)   185
Craig Edwards (16)   186
Becki Callander (15)   187
Helena Dellow (17)   188
Verity Falconer (14)   189
Rebecca Stewart (14)   190
Emma Graham (14)   190
Sophie Robeson (15)   191
Victoria Grant (14)   191
Ross Gillie (14)   192
Heather Portsmouth (12)   192
Amy Wilson (15)   193
John Grant (12)   193
Fiona Hunter (15)   194
Daniel Bennet (12)   194
Kirsty Thomson & Emma Coleman (16)   195
Emily Jones (13)   195
Fionn Page (12)   196
Daniella Pannone (12)   197
Kieran Cook (12)   198
Joni Falla (11)   198
Megan Cuthers (12)   199
Lisa Watson (13)   199
Amy Dodds (12)   200
Melanie King (11)   201
Sean Robson (14)   202

Kirkintilloch High School, Kirkintilloch
Rachael O'Rourke (13)   202
Jack Butler (12)   203
Katrina Hope (13)   203
Emma Kinney (12)   204
Kim-Michal Blythe (13)   205
Laura Wylie (13)   206
Jonathan Fitzpatrick (12)   207
Taylor Kindred (13)   208

Loudoun Academy, Galston

Merchiston Castle School, Edinburgh

Roman Kermani (12)   235
Andrew Spears (12)   236
Andrew Boyd (12)   236
Michael Nicol (12)   237
Rory McMenigall (11)   237
Harry Clark (13)   238
David Black (12)   238
Matthew Gorrie (13)   239
Jamie Stewart (14)   240
Alex Ruff (13)   240
Emilio Maurer (14)   241
Craig Lumsden (13)   241
Hugh Bambridge (12)   242
Ruaraidh Drummond (12)   242
Lazaro Hernandez (14)   243
James Gell (11)   243
Harry Fletcher (13)   244
George Erlanger (11)   244
Dougie Duff (13)   245
Angus Lindsay (11)   245
Adam Linton (11)   246
Kyle Smith (13)   247
Hamilton McMillan (13)   248
Edward Henderson-Howat (11)   248
Tim Balfour (12)   249
Ben Erlanger (14)   250
Angus Paterson (11)   251
Marinus Maris (14)   252
Campbell Paton (13)   253
Rob Dickson (11)   253
Jaime Arroyo (13)   254
Vlad Mackenzie (11)   254
Kerr Aitken (13)   255
Grant Hardie (13)   255
Nathan Kupisz (11)   255
Justin Chu (13)   256

Oakbank School, Aberdeen
Derek Hudson (14)   256

Our Lady's High School, Seafar

Snowdon School, Stirling

The Poems

Marie Celeste

The Marie Celeste left New York harbour
On a blazing, sunny day
The 11 people left without a thought
Of ever coming back
They were heading across the sea with a cargo of alcohol
But never managed to get there

On December 5th that dreadful year
Of 1872
A passing ship came sailing by
And saw the ship adrift
They went on board to look about
But found no trace of soul or life

Then the mystery came up
A lifeboat missing, belongings left
And a captain, his wife, a two-year-old kid
And eight crew members all missing from the ship
They hunted high, they hunted low
But they could find no evidence
Of where the people had gone.
The ship was as dead as a graveyard.

Samuel Stewart (12)
Alness Academy, Alness

Black

Black is an evil power which leads to the cause of death
It is in graveyards in the pure darkness
Gravestones look like witches' hats
The mysterious night sky
Black is the thunder, gothic sky
Black is the sign of holiness.

Martin Wunder (12)
Alness Academy, Alness

Marie Celeste

A ship adrift on December the 5th
In the Atlantic Ocean
Abandoned, ghostly, no sign of life
The haunted howling, high waves hit the Marie Celeste.
The wind howled like a wolf howling aloud.

The dark, dark sky with waves hitting high
At the Marie Celeste
The mist was like ghosts blocking the view
The rain dropping down on my face
As I jumped off the Marie Celeste.

The history before the Marie Celeste was
That two boats went missing
On December the 5th last year before the Marie Celeste
Eight crew members and a captain aboard went missing
A lifeboat afloat and another lifeboat missing in the Atlantic Ocean.

On December the 5th a boat went missing
A lady awaiting to be the queen and a captain called Benjamin.

The Marie Celeste made the front page of the newspapers
All over the world the news went to the people in their homes
And now, today, all year round
No one has thought about the Marie Celeste.

Fiona Brown (12)
Alness Academy, Alness

Scarlet

Long fingers of flames,
Blood lying on the dew-painted grass,
Anger like a pan of soup bubbling over.
A big bus coming towards me,
The lipstick of a lying friend stealing your man,
A big heart beating lovingly:
Scarlet!

Mairi Livesley (12)
Alness Academy, Alness

The Marie Celeste

We went to see what happened that night
When 11 went missing.

A passing boat at midnight brought news of a lonely boat.
The sea felt like ice.

The winter day broke grey and stormy,
With stormy rain and high winds,
As o'er the swell our boat made way as slow as a turtle.

As we neared the lonely ship
The feeling was of being near a ghostly ship.

Yet as we crawled up the ladder
We only saw a table spread for dinner.
Meat and cheese and bread;
But all untouched; and no one there,
As though, when they sat down to eat,
They heard a loud cheeping of a bird.

And, as we listened in the white of the dark living room,
A chill clutched our breath.

We seemed to stand for an endless time.
11 went missing one night.

Jodie Scott (12)
Alness Academy, Alness

Pink

The bright colour stands out.
It is like a lovely rose swaying in the breeze,
Like Barbie dolls on the shelf,
Like a pink sky at night.
Pink is a beautiful colour.

Nicole Murphy (12)
Alness Academy, Alness

Marie Celeste

M any a sailor frightened by its sight.
A bandoned in the deep, blue sea.
R aging winds sweep through the Marie Celeste the whole night.
I see bare shadows raging across the floor.
E erie silence covers the ship.

C old winds scatter across the ship.
E verywhere they go you can hear them screeching on
the floorboards.
L ashing waves smash against the boat.
E veryone is missing from the boat.
S ilent creeks travel across the Marie Celeste.
T errible smells of mouldy bread and cheese.
E verywhere I look there is an empty space apart from a
flittering map and a ticking clock.
Tick-tock, tick-tock.

Stephen McGaw (12)
Alness Academy, Alness

I Thought . . .

I thought it was Saturday today.
I thought I wouldn't have to go to school.
I thought I could have a lie-in this morning.
I thought about all of the things I was going to do.
I thought about all of the time I had to enjoy myself.
I thought about how good it was that I was in good health.
I thought that it was Saturday this morning.
I thought so terribly wrong.
As now I have realised that it is Thursday today.
I shall have to go to school.
No long lie-in for me on a school day.
I'm beginning to feel unwell!

Mairi Ferrier (12)
Alness Academy, Alness

Mysterious Marie Celeste

The Marie Celeste it stopped like a clock
From the Marie Celeste the lifeboat did drop
It stopped like a clock and plunged to the sea
The Marie Celeste we never will see

I took my first step on this mysterious boat
It smelled like mouldy beans and lots of old folk
Nothing was missing, it was all still there
All that happened was a knocked down chair

I looked to the distance and all I could see
Was a lifeboat afloat on the deep, blue sea
The ship was empty to my surprise
But everything was there, I couldn't believe my eyes

It is still a mystery what happened to the crew
But the Marie Celeste works like new
The Marie Celeste it stopped like a clock
From the Marie Celeste the lifeboat did drop

It stopped like a clock and plunged to the sea
The passengers of the Marie Celeste we never will see!

Samantha May McGuinness (12)
Alness Academy, Alness

Black

Black is a scary death at night-time.
The rats in an empty cage.
The darkness of coal.
Black is a mysterious dungeon,
Dark, damp and dangerous.
Black is the colour of mourning,
Sadness at funerals.
Blackness is the shadow
Over the people who have lied
And been hurtful to others.
Black is evil.

Harriet Shaw (11)
Alness Academy, Alness

Marie Celeste

One stormy evening,
It was dark, dark, dark.
The weather was wet, wild and windy
And it was as silent as the clouds in the night sky.

As we neared the snow-white ship,
And looked up at the towering height,
There was no one on the deck,
There was no one at the helm,
No one.

One lifeboat missing,
All belongings left.
The smell of a roast dinner,
Nothing had been theft.

The waves were as tall as the Eiffel Tower,
Everything was going side to side.
The boat was tipping over,
I'm surprised we never died.

As we listened in the gloom,
We walked through the darkened room,
To find that no one was there,
The whole ship was bare.

Jenna Burgess (12)
Alness Academy, Alness

I Thought

I thought you were my partner
I thought you said you cared
I thought I could depend on you
I thought I could rely on you
I thought you were trusting
I thought you would love me.

Gary Williamson (12)
Alness Academy, Alness

Marie Celeste

One stormy evening
The sky was alight
We steered under the clouds that night
Then we saw adrift that night

The ship had a missing lifeboat
When we approached it
There was no sign of crew
We boarded it

It was unreal
No sign of crew but personal belongings
For overhead the queer, black gulls screeched
The stench on board alone could have killed hundreds

Where are they?
What are they?
Who are they?

We abandoned that ship and boarded ours
We were on our way to shore
And above the same birds screeched

When we all got off the boat we spread the word
Not one soul believed us
We had become nationwide heroes.

Aiden Lowrie (12)
Alness Academy, Alness

Winter

W herever you go
 I n winter
N o matter where you go
 T he mountains will have snow
 E verest to Alps, snow on top
 R ain frozen makes snow.

Peter Cooper (12)
Alness Academy, Alness

My Marie Celeste Poem

Spooky and mysterious,
Lifeless and limp.
Ghostly and ghastly,
Abandoned.

Everything, everything, everything gone,
What could have happened?
What went wrong?

The gloomy, sooty fog.
Don't know if it's night or day.
As we go near the boat,
Our boat starts to sway.

No sunlight comes through,
Those sooty, grey clouds.
Cargo still loaded on the ship.
All is still there.

Wandering and wondering,
What could be true?
What's the true story?
What can we do?

No storm in the sea,
My spine gets shivers.
The ship looks dead,
Silence.

We find the belongings,
Of the family and crew.
A puzzled expression on my face,
I haven't got a clue.

The ghostly air catches my breath,
In the air I smell the death.
What really happened to the Marie Celeste?
Did the people die?
Did they kill each other?
I can't confess.

Ami Davidson (12)
Alness Academy, Alness

The Mystery Of The Marie Celeste

Sailing silently across the dark sea,
Something was soundlessly waiting for me.
A ship, deserted, not a soul there,
Endlessly floating in the middle of nowhere.

I rowed to the ship and clambered on board,
I'd no idea what I was heading toward.
The deck lay bare, dust blew about
'Is anyone here?' I heard myself shout.

The wind whistled, the ship creaked,
The waves started to grow.
The more I investigated,
The more I wanted to know.

I searched and searched,
But found only some crates of beer.
Then from the corner of my eye,
I spotted something quite queer.

It moved like the wind,
It was as loud as a truck.
It flew right through me,
My final hour had struck.

I opened my eyes,
The sun shone bright.
I kept wondering and wondering,
What happened last night?

I left the ship,
But didn't feel alone.
I felt that night
There was more I should've known.

I've never been the same,
Since I saw that thing fly.
But the last thing I remember,
Is its cold, cruel eye.

Laura Barry (12)
Alness Academy, Alness

The Mystery Of The Marie Celeste

As we drew nearer the cold air
Got even colder, the silhouette became clear
The object was a ship
The air was like a ghostly presence
The ship sat sadly in the sea
We sailed closer, our anchor dropped
The other ship bobbed
We climbed on the other ship
To investigate, I tasted fear
I felt all trembly and cold
I looked around, the cargo still there
All in one piece
Nothing touched, then I noticed it
A lifeboat, it wasn't there
The crew all gone too
The atmosphere was like a cold graveyard
Full of haunting ghosts
I felt a feeling of sadness fall over me
The ship floated as if it were magical
The sky got darker and the heavens opened
On the mystery of the Marie Celeste
The sails billowed in the breeze
I looked over the side to look for damage
All I saw was the slippery-looking refection
Of the moon in the dark, scary sea
A wave hit violently swaying the boat
What happened to the crew?
I don't understand
How could a ship so beautiful
Be left on its own in the middle of the sea?
What happened on that night is a mystery unknown
No one knows
But for years to come
The breeze will blow
And we might not know
The mystery of the Marie Celeste.

Eilish Fraser (12)
Alness Academy, Alness

The Marie Celeste

Nine men aboard the Marie Celeste
A woman and child too.
Though their life is not the best
They keep on powering through.

Awake to see the sky so blue
To see the sun rise
Bright, pure and true.

In that morning, the start of the day
Something would happen, too dreadful to say.

As we approached the drifting boat
We wondered and wondered
And thought and thought.

Was it an illness
Or maybe a fight?
What could have happened
In the dim sunlight?

How many had the boat been lying?
Floating along and quietly sighing.

The boat was a body on the water
Along with the crewmen
The mother and daughter.
What dreadful fate consumed the crewmen?
Will it happen again?

Steven J Baikie (11)
Alness Academy, Alness

Winter

W alking in wonder
 I n the snow
N ow Santa's on his way
T o bring toys
E veryone's in bed
R eady for tomorrow.

Natasha Ross (11)
Alness Academy, Alness

Marie Celeste

One sunny, calm afternoon,
The wind whistled silently,
The sky was as clear as crystals,
You could see for miles in all directions,
Then unexpectedly we came across a ship,
The sails were still up flapping in the whistling wind,
The waves gently rolled and rolled and rolled.

As we neared the ship,
We watched it,
As the ship silently sat all alone,
In the middle of the ocean,
Bobbing up and down in the waves.

As we came alongside it,
The silence was lonely,
As we climbed aboard,
There was no one to be seen,
On the silent, swaying ship,
We searched and searched and searched,
But we still could not find anyone aboard.

The odd thing was,
There was a lifeboat missing,
As well as the captain, his wife, his daughter and eight crew,
But everything else was untouched.

Still, to this day,
No one knows what really happened,
To the mysterious ship,
The Marie Celeste.

Lorna Brown (12)
Alness Academy, Alness

Marie Celeste

The Marie Celeste is still a mystery,
But I can tell you what I did see.
A big blob afloat in the gloom,
But I thought we had best go,
It will be nightfall soon.

But something told me to turn back,
And have a look.
But the way this thing moved,
It gave me the spooks.

As we neared the blob
I could finally see,
It was a ship,
'A *ship*,' we shouted with glee.

As I stepped on the ship
There was a strong smell
Of rotten eggs with beans
And everything old.

Everything was untouched
But a lifeboat was missing,
I wondered what happened
To the crew out drifting.

What happened to the crew
I just don't know,
What happened to the lifeboat?
They must have had a go.

The Marie Celeste is a mystery.
What happened to the crew who were lost at sea?

Emma McAlinden (11)
Alness Academy, Alness

War Is A Waste

W hat a waste war is.
A few thousand men and women
R eady to go and fight for their country

I s it all a big game?
S ome people say it is

A game with no point

W hy must people kill each other for no reason?
A mass murder of innocent lives
S o many lives lost
T here is no end to it
E very day it continues.

Duncan Stove (13)
Brae High School, Brae

Honourable Horrible

H onourable or horrible,
O nly a sham,
L ooks like it's easy,
L ooking like they're fighting to a funky jam,
Y ou want the good guy to win,
W ith his beautiful woman sidekick,
O therwise you would leave,
O nly because you didn't like it,
D own to Earth, none is true,

W ith weapons you can't run and shoot,
A ll the fantasy that will never be,
R eality bites, if you ask me!

Joel Robinson (13)
Brae High School, Brae

Me

As I look in the mirror I laugh at my face
Tired-looking, hair a mess
I look a disgrace
The only good thing, the way I dress

At my ugliness I sigh
I look once more, I cry
I clear away my tears
I head out to face all my fears

As I look in the mirror I laugh at my face
Tired-looking, hair a mess
I look a disgrace
The only good thing, the way I dress

Tired-looking, hair a mess
At my ugliness I sigh
The only good thing, the way I dress
I look once more, I cry

At my ugliness I sigh
I clear way my tears
I look once more, I cry
I head out to face all my fears

I clear away my tears
I look a disgrace
I head out to face all my fears
As I look in the mirror I laugh at my face.

Amy Macpherson (13)
Clydebank High School, Clydebank

What You Think Doesn't Matter

I don't care what you think of me.
I'm just me, nothing more, nothing less.
Don't try to change me!
I don't care if you think I'm a mess.

I'm just me, nothing more, nothing less.
Think what you want, but I won't care.
I don't care if you think I'm a mess.
I won't care even if you stare.

Think what you want but I won't care.
I don't care what you say.
I won't care even if you stare.
You can't mould me like clay.

I don't care what you say.
Don't try to change me!
You can't mould me like clay.
I don't care what you think of me.

Chloë Brown (13)
Clydebank High School, Clydebank

Suicide Will

All week I get dirty looks
I get laughed at, made fun of all day
My only chance to escape is with books
In this hell, should I stay?

I get laughed at, made fun of all day
Will I take my life?
In this hell, should I stay?
Die as an old, depressed wife?

Will I take my life?
My depression is caving in
Die as an old, depressed wife
Am I invisible if no one talks to me?

My depression is caving in
My only chance to escape is with books
Am I invisible if no one talks to me?
All week I get dirty looks.

Anna Brittain (13)
Clydebank High School, Clydebank

The 5 Senses

Red, yellow, blue, green,
All of these colours make a beautiful scene.
Purple, black, white, grey,
All of these colours make a very dull day.

Ding, dong, bang, ring,
The sound of music encourages me to sing.
Play your drum kit as loud as you can,
And listen to the sound of a sizzling frying pan.

Feel the power, feel the force,
But feel the pain when you get a divorce.
Run your taps, hot and cold,
Feel the pressure of your pottery mould.

The bitterness of beer makes me shed a tear,
The sourness of a lemon makes me sneer.
The sweet taste of candy and cakes,
These are all things that I love to intake.

Smelling food makes me feel good,
But when your meal is burnt the smell of smoke makes you choke.
Onions and peppers generate a sneeze,
Oh! How food is a big tease.

Daniel Pearson (14)
Elgin High School, Elgin

15 Things I Love About Him

I love the smell of his hair
I love the smell of his clothes
I love the smell of his neck
As he pulls me close.

I love the way he makes me stare
I love the way he flicks his hair
I love the way he looks at me
Letting me know he cares.

I love the feel of his hand in mine
I love the feel of his fingers running through my hair
I love the feel of his body close to mine
When he hugs me goodbye.

I love the sound of his whispers in my ear
I love the sound of his laugh
I love the sound of his heart beating
As I rest my head on his chest.

I love the taste of his Diesel cologne
I love the taste of his minty-fresh toothpaste
I love the taste of his lips
That's when my heart flips.

Joanne Henderson (14)
Elgin High School, Elgin

Them!

They come out at night,
To give you a fright!
They come out at day,
Who knows who will be their next prey?

Venture into the depths of Hell,
Hear the ringing of a distant church bell!
Face your fear, face your destiny,
The sound of moans are getting close to me!

Their big, red eyes stand out on their face,
My God, their personal hygiene is a disgrace!
Their razor-sharp fangs glow in the dark,
If you are bitten you're cursed with a mark!

Keep your endurance high,
Or you'll be saying goodbye!
Remember to run home,
When you hear the sound of their groan!

When they come in your house,
And you hear the shriek of your cat,
Run to your closet and pick up your bat!
Swing like crazy, knock off their heads,
When you still hear them groaning,
You'll realise they are the living dead!

Dean Higgins (14)
Elgin High School, Elgin

Love!

We go together like strawberries and cream,
So don't ruin my lifelong dream,
Let's make a start that never ends,
I don't just want to be friends.

Love is a deadly poison,
Which can get really annoying,
Attached to someone forever,
With the touch of a feather.

Then when love deteriorates,
You feel you can't deal with it,
When he starts to like you too,
You know he wants to be with you.

Looking across the gleaming sand,
The guy I love grabs my hand,
Can it be happening, can it be true?
Cuddled up here, lying with you,

Why in the world would you pick me?
There's so much better, can't you see?
A pretty picture, hidden treasure,
Waiting to be with you forever.

Wedding bells ringing,
The orchestra dinging,
Love blossoming like flowers,
Together forever, countless hours.

Katie Dunbar (14)
Elgin High School, Elgin

A Hungry Dream

Strawberries, caramel and chocolate ice cream,
Syrup on pancakes, everyone's dream,
Some like it sour, some like it sweet,
But everyone loves a nice, tasty treat.

Shortbread is baking, how can I tell?
The door is wide open, in comes the smell,
Toasties, pizzas and fish and chips,
My nose starts to tingle as I lick my lips.

I sit waiting for the oven to ping!
Can't wait: hear the crunch the spring roll brings,
Pop, pop, pop! That's my popcorn,
Between this and biscuits I am torn.

I press the cake down and it springs back up,
The icing sits waiting in a nice, big cup,
The smooth, sticky icing passes my lips,
If only it didn't go to my hips.

The frothy cream, now piled up high,
The sight of it: so tempting, I'm going to die,
If only it was a chocolate factory; *mmm*, what a scene,
Oh no, not again: it was only a dream.

Aileen Phillips (14)
Elgin High School, Elgin

Out The Grave

The moon is at its full,
Howls can be heard by fools,
Out of their graves they are coming,
Chasing people who are running.

Screams can be heard from the town,
Innocent people falling down.
Blood can be seen all over the ground,
Petrified villagers falling down.

Everybody looks like they are dead;
On the ground are rolling heads.
They are coming towards me;
This is not the way it's supposed to be.

Go to the gun shack in a hurry,
They are closing in and I'm starting to worry.
Get a shotgun and quickly fire,
Oh no, I shot my car tyre.

They are falling down but rising again,
It's now I wish I had a secret den.
Out of ammo - I need a new gun;
This is definitely not what I call fun.

I've found some ammo and put it in,
Start shooting at their shins.
Now I hear the church bell ring,
And they are suddenly vanishing.

Run to the church, get holy water,
Going to be out of a whole load of bother.
Now they have stopped moving forward,
Shoot to prove I'm no coward.

Turned into ooze, formed a giant thing,
Now I need the church bells to ring.
Kicks and punches, I'm being hit,
I'm going to be torn into tiny bits!

Paul Graham (14)
Elgin High School, Elgin

Friend Or Foe?

A friend or foe?
I do not know
I tell her a secret
But can she keep it?

A friendly smile
Might last a while
The kindness she lacks
Speaking behind my back

School I dread
Rumours have spread
In the halls
Names are called

I meet her eye
I wish she'd die
Pain she caused
Behind closed doors

A friend or foe?
I do not know
I told her a secret
She could not keep it.

Claire Smith (14)
Elgin High School, Elgin

Searching

The moon high up in the sky,
The ground beneath my feet,
Looking for a friend of mine,
Trying to evade the foe,
I look for an injured friend,
To come and take her home.

The silence pounding in my ears,
My heart is beating fast,
A light goes out somewhere near,
I hope my friend will last.

Venturing through alleys,
A wind whispers around,
The shadows mix and blend into one,
Her fate will soon be bound.

A distant cry of an alley cat,
A faint whimper of pain,
I follow, I'm close
Hold on,
I will be your saint.

Ann-Marie Siddle (14)
Elgin High School, Elgin

From Good To Bad

'With the help of telescopic eyes,
Someone can see beyond the sky,'
Emma Salem once said.

Who'd ever thought there would be flying cars,
Or telescopic eyes that could see past Mars?

Who'd ever thought the world would freeze over,
Right from Elgin down to Dover?

Everything was fine,
Tall buildings were sublime.

Then it rained and poured,
Now the world is no more.

Victoria McIntosh (14)
Elgin High School, Elgin

The 5 Senses

When you're racing over jumps on a bike.
The sound of music.
When you hear the rain hitting the ground.
The taste of an Indian freshly made.
The touch of snow slowly melting in your hand.
The sight of bikes going past.
The feel of the ball as you kick it.
The sight of your favourite clothes all dirty.
The taste of chocolate melting slowly.
Cars racing past so fast and noisy.
When the wind's behind you on a bike.
The sight of girls walking past.
The taste of freshly-baked bread.
The smell of bacon being cooked.
The taste of cream cakes on your lips.
The feel of being dirty.
The noise of people laughing.
The feel of being on the back of a motorbike.

Greg Shevill (12)
Fortrose Academy, Fortrose

My Favourite Seasons

Oh I hate winter! The cold's like a splinter at minus 12
I shout out loud, 'When will the sun come out?'
The snow blankets everything the eye can see
Oh the cold touch of wind as you shiver, as your hands turn blue.
Oh, winter, I hate you!

Oh spring, not too hot, not too cold.
As new life is made we have a fresh start.
Oh, spring, I love you!
As leaves start to grow and the snow starts to go.
All is bright and everything's alright
And the sound of trees swaying in the breeze
And all birds talk in their trees
Singing a sweet-sounding tune.
Oh, spring, I love you.

Oh summer, season of drought and dehydration.
It's too hot.
With suncream on and the scorching laser ray of the sun.
With your top off, blisters on shoulders.
Oh, summer, I hate you.
When crops don't grow and famine doesn't go
And summer really makes its point.
Oh, summer, I hate you.

Oh autumn, lovely autumn.
Not too hot, not too cold.
Oh, autumn, I love you.
When trees turn into colours and leaves fall off trees
And winter is coming.
Oh, autumn, I love you.
When all is fine
And plants are divine
As the sun sets on a warm, autumn's night.
Oh, autumn, I love you.

Josh Cartwright (12)
Fortrose Academy, Fortrose

Things I Love

I love jumping walls on my bike until it breaks.
Looking at good-looking girls.
Listening to my music.
I love the smell of burning wood.
But I love my girlfriend even more.
I love the smell of petrol.
I love playing football.
I love spearmint Polos.
I also love Rolos.
I love running around in fresh air.
Once I got chased by a bear.
I love my mum, my granny, my dad and his car
And all my family.
I love my computer, my TV and my bed . . .
And the colour red.
I love the word sheesht
But not the word weesht.

David Fair (12)
Fortrose Academy, Fortrose

Painting Possibilities

A lone line sweeps with grace across the white,
Is it a hill or could it be a face?
A second stroke removes the phrase 'it might',
While third and fourth reveal a quiet place
Surrounded by a jagged, white-topped range
Of mountains that touch opal, patterned skies.
In my mind the willows from green change,
And silver spearheads writhe before my eyes.
Then through the paper window I can see
A sheet of glass-like water that reflects
The forest that grows in the mountain's lee,
And leaves that on the forest floor collect.
When paper, dagger-pointed graphite meets,
A single line can many scenes repeat.

Johann Dunn (14)
Fortrose Academy, Fortrose

Lions Led By Donkeys

Like a symphony the barrage of artillery fire erupted with sound,
In waves the orchestra would rise to a cacophony,
Then fall silent while in the distance their music would pound.

The mission was straightforward,
To take the German lines,
The artillery had wiped out any resistance, that was sure.

Captain Rodger said good luck to us and sent us on our way,
I thought this odd for we did not need luck,
The Jerries would have abandoned their posts and scarpered.

Then without warning the symphony rose to an aching chord,
The pounding grew relentless,
The air became increasingly saturated with sound,

And then it stopped,
A skylark sang a graceful song,
That had only three notes and yet endless variety of interval.

This ceasefire was the signal,
A high-pitched whistle sounded,
And the long, meandering line of men began shuffling forward.

Up and over the trench wall we edged,
Out of the dank and stench-filled trenches we emerged
Proud and determined,
900 yards of no-man's-land separated us from our objective.

Much rather than being depressed by the surrounding environment,
I felt most contented and unperturbed,
The warmth of the French July sun brought life to our damp limbs.

Then when entering the area
Where the shells had been raining down,
A shroud of thick, choking smoke engulfed us,
Alarm bells sounded in my head.

With dull thuds men fell to the ground moaning and writhing in pain,
Non-existent machine gun nests opened fire at close proximity,
Scattered around lay corpses peppered with bullet holes -
Lions led by donkeys.

Neil Paul (14)
Fortrose Academy, Fortrose

In A Land

In a land where the sun is a cruel master,
The brass bell rings proudly,
Calling to the small, dark ears of children
Playing in the scorching, inescapable heat.

Into class 4, where the bare, concrete walls offer comfort and cool.

Leave hoes, spades and sacks at the door. 'Morning, madam!'

Tiny, lean behinds shoot to the dusty ground,
Creating clouds of choking particles
That rise and enter tired lungs and yearning stomachs.

Flick through the yellow pages of 'My Work Jotter',
Fingering each with delicate precision.

Through the patterned, concrete window,
The sun casts its merciless glare upon fields of maize.

Inside, the overpowering smell of Earth
Combined with the sweat of enthusiasm
Is ignored as Madam begins teaching.

Aching muscles, empty stomachs
And tightly packed bodies are forgotten,
Instead words, numbers and songs flood the mind
And shut out the world outside.

Rise to sing, rise to pray, and rise to share out textbooks.

Miles away in the west,
Where the sun is a less familiar acquaintance,
We sit, arms folded and faces blank.

Sarah Hulks (17)
Fortrose Academy, Fortrose

The Hallowed Turf

Awareness creeps through the veins
Awareness of the vast crowd's everlasting chants and songs
Awareness of the leathery upper sole of my comfy boots
Awareness of the smells of burgers and hotdogs
Wafting onto the freshly-cut, hallowed turf
Awareness of the tension between the two sets of fans

Feelings creep into the pit of the stomach
Feelings of anticipation
Feelings of fear
Feelings of tension you could
Cut
With a
Knife
Most of all, however, feelings of pride

Sights fill the eyes
Sight of seas of blue, red and white
Sights of legions of green
Sights of men, women and children
Who have turned out to see their beloved team play
Sights of the Saltire, the Union Jack and the tricolours of
Green
White
And orange
Fill the stadium

Sounds of the captain's encouragement enters the ears
Sounds of the manager's motivation ring in the memory
Sounds of the bands and music playing on the speakers
And finally . . .
The sound of the whistle.

David Manson (14)
Fortrose Academy, Fortrose

Sonnet To Josie

When I'm lonely and no one's there to see,
When all the comfort in the world has gone,
Then you come in and come and rescue me,
Blossoms bloom on trees and birds sing along.
Then you flew to France leaving me alone,
Life is dull and boring when you're away,
You didn't e-mail me when I was home,
And you didn't call when I was astray.
The blossom has withered, the trees are dead,
The grass stopped growing; the wells have gone dry,
She'll write - just be patient - that's what she said,
Why didn't you call? I'm asking you why?
Why did you do this? You're driving me mad!
When you get back the punishment is bad.

Catriona MacNally & Isbel Pendlebury (14)
Fortrose Academy, Fortrose

Sonnet J

When I behold thine eyes I feel true love,
Thou art more beautiful than Eve herself,
Thou art as fair as the white-feathered dove,
If thou were Santa I would be thine elf,
Many Jasons come in a quest for thee,
Yet I hope I would be the one you choose
To unlock your heart, do I need a key?
When I first saw you my spirit arose,
Heaven surrounds thee when thou walkest past,
You'll dazzle me for all eternity,
I fear the day when I shall see you last,
Your life to me is quite compulsory,
Your golden locks glimmer in the sunlight,
My heart treasures you, don't take off in flight.

Nial Deveney & Alex Cooper (14)
& Magnus Davidson
Fortrose Academy, Fortrose

I Love

I love these:
Crunchy snow on a winter's day
And rain and grey clouds.
Warm cakes with cherries
Icing left to cool.
My sister's smell.
When I get to see them,
Pebbles dropping into water
Slowly, quietly.
My hand softly stroking the smooth surface of calm water.
My dog so pleased to see me when I come home panting, jumping.
The sweetish smell of hot chocolate and chocolate itself
Melting in your mouth.
Orchestras getting ready to perform, tuning the instruments to play.
Rough texture of wood on trunks or branches.
I will always love these.

Jessica Bates (12)
Fortrose Academy, Fortrose

The Pizza

Your big, round face fills me with joy,
I stare at you, my taste buds tingling,
You're ten times better than your cheap, free toy,
I'd rather be with you than out mingling,
As I lean in I want you more and more,
You look so nice in your pineapple dress,
But as I reach out there's a knock at the door,
I run to the door filled with distress,
Everyone here wants to share you,
I scream, 'She's mine, she's mine, leave here now!'
But it's too late, I hit them with my shoe,
I hit them hard, *kapow, kapow, kapow,*
I never did get back my new shoe,
But it was worth it, you gorgeous pizza you.

Rebecca Rennie (13) & Robin Shilland (14)
Fortrose Academy, Fortrose

Silver Sunshine

Things that I love:
Fast cars zooming
Loud music booming
Hot chocolate simmering
A fruity, fig yoghurt, nice and cold
Mint ice cream
Yum, yum
Chips and curry sauce, nice and warm
Birds in the morning waking me up
Spare ribs cooking in the oven
Wasps and bees buzzing in the breeze
Playing football is so much fun
Sound of fireworks going *bang, bang, bang*
Which light up the sky in different colours
The atmosphere at a football match
All the crowd shouting for their favourite football team
Crouching down to see the grass
And all the things that live on the vegetation
The skin of oranges is so rough
It is like a dirt road
Deer crossing the moor, so beautiful but even better in the snow
At night when the sun goes down and the sky is red
It is like an artist's palette.

Billy Mackenzie (11)
Fortrose Academy, Fortrose

Aimee

The heavy hospital door slowly swung open
Revealing a baby, swaddled in white
Her fairy-like fingers wrapped around mine
Small and delicate
Grip firm
Her face lost in dreams
Yet those delicate fingers held more strength
Than my body or even my mind could withdraw from

My little sister

Our old kitchen door groaned on its hinges
Behind it sat a toddler in a highchair
The remains of a bourbon biscuit
Lay crumbled around a mischievous grin
Toes were clarted in a lumpy chocolate paste
Wriggling worms in a puddle of mud

My little sister

Now as I open my bedroom door
I find a young adult at the age of seven
Swinging her legs beneath the toilet pan
'Reading' the Herald Magazine
A Christmas carol hollering from her throat
In the middle of summer

My little sister.

Dawn Coulshed (14)
Fortrose Academy, Fortrose

Lovely Day

Tiny robin redbreast, sitting on his toes.
Hopping, hopping on the crisp, white snow.
Happy, happy as he goes.

Spiky Christmas tree, with scent and golden.
From the kitchen the whiff of turkey on the go.
A glass of grape juice makes me perky.

Sweet sound of carols in the distance.
The parcels all sitting, stacked up high
With shiny ribbons and bright paper,
Waiting to be attacked.

Bang! Bang! There goes a cracker.
Laughing, cheering, happy people.
Glowing candles flickering wildly.
Christmas pudding, hot and sticky.

Drop, drop. The snow is gently falling.
Cold and frosty, the day is closing.
Snuggled up warm in front of the log fire.

Katie Mackay (12)
Fortrose Academy, Fortrose

These Have I Loved

The taste of chocolate melting in my mouth
When I'm in an aeroplane going south
The sight of fireworks when they burst out into the sky
The taste of a packet of Skittles, all the colours like a rainbow
The sound of a bird chirping when it's sitting in the sunshine
The smell of the sea
The sound of a buzzing bee
The touch of the velvet on my mum's coat
Hearing all the waves when I'm out in a boat
The touch of the colourful cat's fur
The smell of the washing powder my mum puts on my clothes
The taste of chips when they are covered in ketchup
The smell of the poisoning petrol going up my nose
The touch of the white, shiny snow melting in my hand
The touch of the golden, glittering sand
The sound of people clapping when you win a prize
The touch of a snake as if it's a scaly sponge
When I'm out on my trampoline jumping as high as the clouds
The taste of the cross curry waiting on the plate
And last but not least
My family.

Anna Forbes (11)
Fortrose Academy, Fortrose

My Favourite Things

Hot chocolate swilling about in your mouth,
Friendly music on your CD player,
Soft, fluffy teddies that you could cuddle all day long,
The smell of baking in the kitchen,
Sound of bubblewrap being popped.
It's like fireworks banging in the sky.
Fireworks with a loud bang
And all their pretty colours.
Smelly perfume that smells like strawberries,
A chocolate bar melting on your tongue
And swilling around your mouth.
A huge Christmas tree
With lots of lights and tinsel,
Sparkling all around . . .
With chocolate treats on top.
Spearmint Polos with a hint of peppermint,
A big, widescreen TV
With Sky and a DVD player.
A soft, fluffy, white rabbit with floppy ears,
A box of cinnamon TicTacs (winter warmers)
Which are as hot as a fire.

Lauren Urquhart (12)
Fortrose Academy, Fortrose

Tasting

Going to a football match is my favourite thing
While people in the crowd cheer and sing
Going home with a Rangers top and feeling glad
When you lose, it's not so bad
I love the smell of melting macaroni
And the feel of soft, sticky dough
With a taste of pasta
And a smear of boiling curry sauce
I have some model cars
Which I push along the floor
They are fast and cool
And they are to adore
I like the sound of bubblewrap
Like kids popping poppers
I like them so much
Because they remind me of fireworks
I like the taste of toffee
And chocolate in your mouth
And tea at night
Just before bed
When I'm tucked up tight.

Adam McBean (12)
Fortrose Academy, Fortrose

These Have I Loved

These have I loved:
Looking out
Of the window seeing the mountains
Covered in soft, friendly snow
The loud sound of fireworks cracking
And bursting in the midnight sky
The taste of chocolate
Sweeties melting in my mouth
The soft touch of my cat's
Fur, like velvet when I pet it
The smell of mum's
New perfume when she walks past me
When I lie in the sun and
Look at the rainbow
In the blue sky. I like
To lie in bed and listen
To the water
Dripping off the roof tiles
I like to wake up in the morning and look
Out the window and watch
The running rabbits fight and play in the
Long, green grass
I like to listen to the sea
Coming into the rocky rocks
The sweet smell of hot
Baked bread
Out of the steaming oven
I like the hot, spicy taste
Of chicken curry
Heating in my mouth
I love when I walk down stairs
On Christmas morning and
See all my presents under
The Christmas tree.

Jennie McCallum (11)
Fortrose Academy, Fortrose

Things I Like

I like to see fast cars go zooming past
And the deer running joyfully across the hills without a worry.
The sound of the brakes squeak
Like a little mouse running through a house
Also the taste of luxurious chocolate when it melts in your mouth
And the taste of warm, fresh, friendly bread
And a plate of good old mince and tatties
I also like to hear the loud purr of a boy racer car
And the roar of the exhaust
I like the smell of irresistible fresh baking
I like the touch of a snake
It feels like a very dry sponge
And my hamster Casper
He is so soft and feels like a nice, fluffy cotton wool.

Arran Scobbie (11)
Fortrose Academy, Fortrose

Things From The Heart

Chocolate cake fresh out of the oven
Steaming and gleaming on the tray
Cat fur like smooth silk sweeping along your arm
Sunshine creeping through the silent clouds
Soft, fluffy teddies like cat fur
And the relaxing sound of my cat's purr
The strong smell of petrol rushing through the petrol pump
Ronaldo running down the pitch trying to score against Ipswich
Pancakes fresh from the pan
Smothered in butter then dripping in jam
The beat of the music in my ear
James Blunt I like to hear
When I have time I love to watch 'Hollyoaks', 'Corrie', 'Casualty'
Sweet sweeties - Galaxy, Flake
Waiting for me to eat them up.

Lisa Greenwood (12)
Fortrose Academy, Fortrose

Untitled

I love the sound of the birds breaking out of the trees
Leaves rustling restlessly on the ground.
Sunlight goes over the country hills
And the full moon glares down at us.
Footsteps silently striding down the road
With the moonlight streaming through the trees at him.
Owls screeching in the moonlit trees.
Deer darting in and out of the bushes
Away from danger.
The sudden sound of a rapid rifle
Echoes through the tiny forest.
Silence follows the shot.
Minutes go by in the deathly silence.
Ears strain, noses twitch, eyes widen with fear.
Hearts hammering.
No sign of death comes to them this time.
Breaking branches. Danger leaves the forest.
Parents return to their young.
Noise picks up as animals return to normal.
The sun rises slowly again up over the hills
Ending the night's activities.
A fresh start with birds singing the dawn chorus.

Calum Munro (12)
Fortrose Academy, Fortrose

My Favourite Things

Sunset like a big, orange ball
Sitting behind a lit up hill;
Fat, juicy strawberries laying
Lazily on a white plate;
The sound of autumn leaves
Crackling, crunching on the ground
While people run through them;
Lovely, soft, fluffy teddies laughing
On a child's bed;
Chocolate melting in your mouth like
A river of your favourite food
Falling down a waterfall;
The sight of hungry horses
Running through a field frantic
To get their food;
Soft chocolate chip cookies
Going round and round in your
Mouth;
Seeing and touching my cool,
Colourful pillows on my bed;
Yummy, yellow bananas bathed
In milk chocolate, cooked slowly
On a barbecue
And photos of my favourite
Friends and family on my bedroom wall.

Marianne Stevenson (11)
Fortrose Academy, Fortrose

Bliss . . .

The smell of fresh, homemade soup
Steaming on the table
The leaves of a willow rustling in the breeze
The sights of Rome
The texture of an ice cream cone
The sparkle of a sunbeam sneaking under a cloud
The bright bloom of spring
Yellow, purple, blue and red
Those are the colours that you see
The sound of the sea and lapping waves
DVDs and videos on a Friday night
Ding, dong! go the bells
To mark the end of the lesson
The sweet taste of chocolate
Melting in the mouth
My dog chasing her tail
Marshmallows and cream
On top of hot chocolate
And last but not least
My family!
Oh . . . my blissful world.

Julie Auld (11)
Fortrose Academy, Fortrose

Rabbits

They jump in the sun
They have some fun
They have floppy ears
So they can't hear
They have fluffy tails
And are scared of snails
Rabbits are the best
Better than the rest!

Natalie Chilvers (12)
Gleniffer High School, Paisley

Chocolate

C reamy and mouth-watering
H azelnut filing
O ld flavours and new flavours
C aramel centres
O bviously it's the best
L ong-lasting (sometimes)
A dream to have in your hand
T o die for
E dible and gorgeous

> As you can see chocolate is great
> It's the nicest thing to put on your plate
> Chocolate is so cool
> As you should know they rule.

Mars, Munchies, Snickers, Lion,
Yorkie, Twirl, Kit-Kat, Twix, Galaxy,
Dairy Milk.

Chloë Anne Watson (13)
Gleniffer High School, Paisley

Ma Bro

Ma big bro is the best.
He's better than all the rest.
When I'm down and sad
He always makes me happy and glad!

He loves me.
I love him.
We love each other.
It's so much fun.

So thank you for being ma bro.
You deserve a medal or even more.

Katie O'Malley (13)
Gleniffer High School, Paisley

Harry Potter

Harry Potter
Is a sorcerer
And my favourite too

Hermione Granger
Isn't a stranger
To the world of knowledge and books

Ronald Weasley
He is queasy
When dealing with spiders and ghouls

They study at Hogwarts
Where evil lurks
And so do witches, wizards and ghosts

Their teacher is Snape
He looks like a snake
But not as bad as Lord Voldemort
Now he looks like a wart

But no matter what movie
One, two, three or four
It will always be Harry
Battling Lord Voldemort.

Jordan Brown (12)
Gleniffer High School, Paisley

Christmas Time

It's Christmas time, *hip, hip, hooray*
All the children going out to play
In the snow so icy and wet
Parents wondering what to get
Children not letting them forget
It's Christmas time, *hip, hip, hooray.*

Grant Alexander McAulay (12)
Gleniffer High School, Paisley

Movies

Movies are so great
But some I hate
I *love* action
Personally I think it's a big attraction
I hate romantics, they're so boring
Half the time I'm on the sofa snoring
At horrors I get the creeps
I just can't get to sleep
I *love* detectives, who's the spy?
You always have to keep a close eye
Comedy, it's *so funny*
Especially when it's about Bugs Bunny
It's also funny when someone says, 'Groovy,'
I think comedy is my favourite movie
You can go to the cinema
Or buy a DVD
That's why movies are the best, they have to be.

Fraser Dalglish (11)
Gleniffer High School, Paisley

Concert Hall, It's A Ball

At a concert we have a ball.
Always in a music hall.
The bands are playing.
The music's loud.
Everyone's swaying in the crowd.
The rhythm has a happy beat.
It makes you want to tap your feet.
Instead the fans just clap their hands
To show that they appreciate the bands.

Ross Carlton (13)
Gleniffer High School, Paisley

Power Of Poetry

P oetry homework so quieten down
O ut of my mind, it's so hard to begin
W hat will I write about? Pet, toy or town?
E lephant stampedes make less of a din
R ushing and running as my thoughts scatter

O ff they go in every direction
F inally coming back a lot fatter

P lease don't disturb, check in at reception
O n and on my thoughts grow even bigger
E verything is working and it all fits
T houghts I keep digging up with my big digger
R ight at the end now, just the last few bits
Y es! I've done it, I've finished my poem.

Paula Milliken (13)
Gleniffer High School, Paisley

About Me

I think I'm kind
I think I'm funny
No you're not
You've got teeth like a bunny
I think I'm smart
I think I'm cool
But you're not
You're nothing but a stupid fool
I think I'm sound
I think I'm clean
All the other kids are very mean
If I say what I think
They put my head down the sink.

Gerry Hainey (13)
Gleniffer High School, Paisley

The Jungle - Or Not

The jungle is big and tall
There are some creatures that are small
There is no electricity
It is nothing like a city
In the camp is where I sleep
But you feel like you are watched by a creep
I thought it was my imagination first
But it came back the next day then I knew
It had a blood thirst
Now I know I have to run
But the creep thinks it's still fun
I felt my feet being pulled away
Then I heard something say,
'Get in and bring in yer ball,'
My back garden is big and small.

John McEwan (13)
Gleniffer High School, Paisley

At The Beach!

The splashing of the water
And goldness of the sand
The noise of children screaming
As they run across the land
And when the sun shines on you
You know what you must do
Put on your sunscreen
Don't go back in the pool!
Time to eat some sandwiches
They're always full of sand
So I may as well get an ice lolly
And go watch the marching band.

Amanda Jamieson (13)
Gleniffer High School, Paisley

My Cold

Thud, thump, throb
A giant jumps on my head
Which is heavy with thoughts.

Splutter, sneeze, swallow
A bogart constricts my throat
Which is thick with phlegm.

Drip, drop, dribble
A snail smears my sleeve
Which is green with slime.

Hot, hellish, humid
A furnace burns my forehead
Which is branded with fever.

Cough, crackle, croak
A hag hampers my breathing
Which is hoarse and wheezy.

Bed, bottle, book
The things I really need
When I'm full of the cold.

Aisling Gilbert (11)
Gleniffer High School, Paisley

Me At The Concert

I love going to concerts
I love the atmosphere
I love the loud music
And I love to cheer
Live and loud is so fun
I love the fair
I love to get a burger in a bun
And it is so bright with all the lights
I love to get a souvenir
I love going to concerts.

Chantal Walker (12)
Gleniffer High School, Paisley

The Sun

When the sun shines it sparkles so bright,
When it glistens it is a wonderful sight,
When it comes out I rise with a shine,
Today's going to be the day that the world will be mine,
When I see the flares coming off the sun,
I say to myself, *now we'll have some fun*,
The electrical sun keeps me going through the day,
And then at night it creeps away.

Fraser Coyle (13)
Gleniffer High School, Paisley

A Hot Summer's Day

The sun is like a hot yellow beach ball.
It is as round as a melon.
The sea is as blue as the clear blue sky.
The sand is as fine as silk.
The grey rocks by the edge are like sleepy seals.
The sun is like hot flames of fire.
Summer is as lovely as Heaven that brightens up the day.

Lorna McIntyre (12)
Gleniffer High School, Paisley

Winter

Falling snow
And the white moon's glow
People carol singing
And ice twinkling
Glittering across the ground
Without a sound
Winter is near
No, winter is here.

Chloë Aitchison (13)
Gleniffer High School, Paisley

The Race Of The Car

A car's engine is the heart
It beats in a way of simplicity
The pistons go up and down with a bang

The grumble of the V8 muscle
The whistle of the supercharger is a high screech of power
As it pulls away at great speed
The back of the car vanishes into a cloud of smoke
As the wheels spin it grabs the road and rips along at great speed.

The finish is fast approaching, the car is miles ahead
As it reaches the finish line the car behind is getting closer
The driver puts his foot to the floor and pips him to the post
Victory at last.

Connor Fulton (12)
Gleniffer High School, Paisley

Life

Life is full of likes and dislikes,
Full of enjoyment and disappointments.
Life is full of fun and homework,
Full of smiles or frowns!

What we do in life today,
Affects what we do in life tomorrow.
It's about the thoughts that we think,
It's about the choices we make.

What are you gonna do with your life today?
What are you gonna do with your life tomorrow?
It's up to you . . .

Ben Gardiner (12)
Gleniffer High School, Paisley

My Crazy Sister

She has strawberry-blonde hair
And she runs around in her underwear
She sometimes tells tales on me
She always knocks over my mum's tea
She usually gets her way
But tomorrow's just another day
But then again I love her so
She's a little witch, I should know
She's like the Devil in disguise
A little girl that's very wise
In her room she plots away
The little devil's name is *Ashleigh.*

David Guthrie (13)
Gleniffer High School, Paisley

Christmas Time

Christmas time is a wonderful time
The crackling of wrapping paper
The jingling of the bells
The soft sound of snow crunching
The noise of children munching
The soft, sweet sound of a choir
Next to a roaring fire
The sizzling sound of Mum cooking the roast
When everyone arrives she stands
And makes a toast
The good old days of Christmas.

Ainsley Boyle (13)
Gleniffer High School, Paisley

Little Sister

My little sister is a devil
She loves to scribble
- on my things.

She thinks that she's smart
- only at messy art

She'll go in a mood
If you don't do what she wants
Then she'll do what you don't want!

That's my lil' sis!

Jennifer Cooney (13)
Gleniffer High School, Paisley

At A Football Match

Bang, boom, bash as the fans cheer their side on.
Chaos as the opposition get out of hand.
The rumble of the feet coming from the stand.
As the ref peeps his whistle for half-time.
Pies, hot dogs, Bovrils, a tasty treat
For all the people sitting in their seats.
The second half gets underway.
Tension mounts, the seconds ticking away.
St Mirren have won and made my day.

Scott Gemmell (12)
Gleniffer High School, Paisley

A Cold Winter Day

The snow is as white as James Cockburn's teeth.
The wind blows as fast as a cheetah.
The trees are as bare as a baby's bottom.
The snowballs are as fast as jets.

Iain McCabe (12)
Gleniffer High School, Paisley

Who Cares?

Who cares for the elderly?
Who cares for the old?
Not many people I've been told.

The eyes are dim and hearing gone
With only their past to think upon.

The Zimmer's there all raring to go.
The problem is their feet are too slow.

Who cares for the elderly?
Who cares for the old?
Not many people I've been told.

Shannon Coubrough (11)
Gleniffer High School, Paisley

My Brother

His eyes are as blue as the sea.
His hair is brown and spiky like a hedgehog.
His voice is loud like an alarm bell.
He always sings to songs on TV.
He is tall and skinny like a rake.
He is always banging about, all you hear is *bang, bang, clatter.*
His legs are long like a jenny longlegs.
He is kind sometimes but at other times he is a wacky wrestler.
That's my wee, daft brother.

Kirsty Crawford (12)
Gleniffer High School, Paisley

Colours

The sky is as blue as the sea.
The grass is as green as a packet of Extra chewing gum.
The sun is as red as a poppy.
The sand is as yellow as the lollipop lady's lollipop stick.

Craig Baxter (12)
Gleniffer High School, Paisley

My Brother

My brother is as tall as a pine tree,
And his eyes are as deep as the deepest, darkest ocean,
He has a brain like the largest, unexplored island,
He has a nose as crooked as a witch's,
And feet as large as a plank of wood,
His arms are as strong as two oxen,
His hair is as thick as a sheep's coat,
His ears are as large as Dumbo's,
His head is as big as two,
My brother is as kind as a deadly crocodile.

Sarah Tweedly (12)
Gleniffer High School, Paisley

Computers!

C *lick, click*
O n it goes
M ove the mouse
P entium 4 processor
U ntidy desk tops
T o the Internet
E nd of your time on the computer
R ead the sign which says
S witch it off.

Fraser Stewart (12)
Gleniffer High School, Paisley

Cars

Cars are so sleek and stylish
The engines are so elegant
The wheels are shiny and silver
The speeds are scary
The grip of the tyres is great
But some cars I hate.

Michael Collins (12)
Gleniffer High School, Paisley

Lost

Where will I go?
What will I do?
Help me please,
I'm lost without you.

Pictures go blurry.
Everything goes furry.
It all looks so funny
Till I realise I'm lost.

Lost,
On my own.
Say a prayer
That you will come back.

I start to cry
As I try
To look for help.
I burn up as if I am going to fry.

Suddenly I see a man,
He says his name is Bob.
He asks what's wrong
As I look forlorn.

I start to sob
All over again
As I confide in Bob.

I look around
On the ground
For you but you're gone.

Where will I go?
What should I do?
Help me please,
I'm lost without you.

Fiona Gemmell (12)
Gleniffer High School, Paisley

Is That The Sound Of Death?

Howling, growling through the night
Giving creatures the fright of their lives
Fangs bared, claws grinding the ground
Howl here, howl there
Is that the sound of death?

Silently down, crackle of leaves
Paws trod on nothing and never leave
Then but slowly comes a piercing cry
Howl here, howl there
Is that the sound of death?

Howling, wincing becomes quiet clear
It comes more clear through the night air
Blood on the trees, nearly everywhere
Howl here, howl there
Is that the sound of death?

Slowly limps down to the lake
Right down here it will not wake
Slowly but steady the wolf lays down
Howl here, howl there
Is that the sound of death?

No one here, not anywhere
It lays down in the middle of nowhere
Lifeless, without a trace
Howl here, howl there
It is the sound of death.

Evelyn Matthew (11)
Gleniffer High School, Paisley

Raging Roller Coasters

The safety bar comes down when you are not ready
Then a sudden jolt
It slowly climbs to the top
Then *zoom, whoosh, loop-the-loop*
Faster and faster
A jolt to the left then to the right
You feel dizzy as the cart is on its side
You begin to enjoy
Then you feel a jolt
The ride is over
You claim that you were not afraid.

Graham Gay (12)
Gleniffer High School, Paisley

The Sapphire Dragon

The dragon has scales as bright as the sun,
She is blue as a sapphire.
Her great, grey eyes see everything,
Her super, spiralling horns as black as night.
When she flies she is always graceful,
She sleeps in creepy caves.
Her spiked, long tail waves from side to side,
Her fire is a weapon,
Burning trees and bushes.
Her teeth are as sharp as daggers,
Her claws like knives.
The great sapphire dragon.

Emma Renton (11)
Gleniffer High School, Paisley

Twilight

The star is an ever-changing gemstone
Turning by the time of day
By midnight it is a diamond
Twinkling in the light
At dawn it is like a topaz
Shining alongside the moon
In the disappearing morning
The emerald winks with a gleam
In the sunset we start to lose the light
The dazzling ruby rises
To bid the world goodnight.

Adam McDermott (12)
Gleniffer High School, Paisley

Behind A Perfect Face

This is my diary
These are my thoughts
This is my life
Or what I've not forgot.

These are my secrets
Rolled up in a box
Tied up with a string
In a tight, double knot.

They're scribbled on paper
With a faded away kiss
Added with a wish
To disappear and not be missed.

My wishes are my prayers
My prayers which lie within
The things that won't go away
Especially when you sin.

Jenny Ferguson (14)
Grove Academy, Broughty Ferry

Reincarnation

My bonsai sitting in the shade
All alone in a desolate place
Lying next to it, a spade
Once a bright red, now a wry face

All alone in a desolate place
I watched its flowers
Once a bright red, now a wry face
Shrivelling up and tumbling towers

I watched its flowers
Dropping away
Shrivelling up and tumbling towers
Death is not romantic, when you see things decay

Dropping away
It's rather simple to understand
Death is not romantic, when you see things decay
Especially when the roots are underhand

It's rather simple to understand
That as the years pass by it becomes romance
Especially when the roots are underhand
But now covered and reduced to an expanse

As the years pass by it becomes romance
As the spot where it once grew
Is now covered and reduced to an expanse
Where the bonsai again grows through and through

As the spot where it once grew
The stalk shoots out, not willing to be swayed
Where the bonsai again grows through and through
My bonsai sitting in the shade.

Alison Wong (14)
Grove Academy, Broughty Ferry

I'm A Celebrity Get Me Out Of Here!

Spiders, ants, bush tucker trials
Campfire songs and sleepless nights
Oh, why on Earth did I come all these miles?
Jumping from helicopters and I don't like heights.

Campfire songs and sleepless nights
Snakes, possums and kangaroos too
Jumping from helicopters and I don't like heights
I would hate to live there, would you?

Snakes, possums and kangaroos too
Rice and beans and kangaroo stew
I would hate to live there, would you?
Public votes narrow us down to a few.

Rice and beans and kangaroo stew
How long will I be here? I cannot tell
Public votes narrow us down to a few
Counting down days until I'm at the hotel.

How long I will be here? I cannot tell
Oh, why on Earth did I come all these miles?
Counting down days until I'm at the hotel
Away from spiders, ants, bush tucker trails.

I'm a celebrity, get me out of here!

Louise Hurrell (13)
Grove Academy, Broughty Ferry

Those Who Are Lost

Those who came before me,
The people I shall not meet,
The knowledge I won't see,
The foes I won't defeat.

The people I shall not meet,
The tales I will never hear,
The foes I won't defeat,
That I will forever fear.

The tales I will never hear,
Memories lost from minds,
That I will forever fear,
The times we cannot find.

Memories lost from minds,
The price we have to pay,
The times we cannot find,
As they die day by day.

The price we have to pay,
For the memories of old,
As they die day by day,
The stories we are told.

For the memories of old,
The time will melt away,
The stories we are told,
When forgotten some day.

The time will melt away,
As the people will not see,
That they cannot stay,
Gone forever from me.

Caitlin McLeish (14)
Grove Academy, Broughty Ferry

Paranoia

I turn the corner,
Met by a hazy mist.
The glowing streetlamps
Shimmering orange off
The frosted pavement.

Footsteps behind me.
I breathe short, sharp, sore breaths.
The cold air so harsh,
My pulse is now racing,
Is it him? I fear.

A strand of my hair
Catches on the withered bush,
As I glance behind me
In expectation of
That sinister figure.

Boldly, I turn round
To face only darkness.
Yet again, too late -
He's escaped, got away,
There's always next time.

Joanne Findlay (14)
Grove Academy, Broughty Ferry

The Death Ship

Ripping through the current, the deadly sea ship sails
Rising out of the dark, the ragged mast
The sails torn and wet, white with a ghostly glow
Crashing through the tumbling waves
Water sloshing and splashing everywhere

Slapping through the twelve-foot waves
As death draws ever closer to the unsuspecting victims
Everything dark, the black of the sky, not a star in sight
Against the grey, choppy sea, where all seems dead
Except the raging anger of the frightful storm . . .

Alex Montgomery (13)
High School of Dundee, Dundee

Fire

As his flaming temper roars through
Room after room,
His fury becoming fiercer and fiercer
He doesn't settle - nor calm
And the eye of the flame never blinks

As his anger climaxes
He lets rip and curses
Burning everything he can touch
Singeing everything in sight
But the eye of the flame never blinks

As he begins to settle
Singeing the door
He has burnt every object
Nowhere to go from here
The eye blinks and the flame disappears.

Rachael Spink (13)
High School of Dundee, Dundee

The Dark Ship

The dark ship draws near
On a blood-red sea
Crashing on the waves
Echoes of the past.

It sails with no crew
Has no destination
Only shadows of death
On a one-way journey
With no turning back.

Surrounded by darkness
And a sea of lost souls
But who is it here for?
Nobody knows.

Jamie Johnston (13)
High School of Dundee, Dundee

The Race

Adrenalin pounding through him, faster than his heart.
His hands are shaking.
His knees are quaking.
He swivels his neck round, eyeing the finishing line.
He challenges it and himself.
Pretending to stretch, he inspects his competition.
Limbering up, they look scared.
But he is not.
He can take it in his stride . . .
Literally.
He peeks at his battered spikes and feels pride.
He's worried, but confident. He's trained hard for this . . .
Rudely cutting into his thoughts the linesman says,
'Marks!'
He jumps up, warms his muscles. He cracks his neck again
And drops to the floor to assume his starting pose.
He breathes shakily and waits for
'Set!'
His back leg automatically extends itself.
It is now steady as is his breathing.
'B!'
Is all he hears of *bang*.
His arms snap back, his body smoothly jerks
Out of his blocks, towards the white ribbon.
His feet are hammering at the track.
His teeth, gritted in determination.
His fleet fly
And over the line he glides
Winning!

Kirsty McEwan (13)
High School of Dundee, Dundee

The Death Ship

A faint shadow coming from the western sunset,
Sailing closer and closer to the battered harbour.
A stench of death curled in the hazy air.
I swore I saw a skeleton! Searching on the lookout tower
But it was lost in the guilty darkness.

It rode high above the waves
That looked smothered in rich, black ink.
There were sails as black as charcoal
That hung tattered being whipped by the northern winds.
I could feel the ghostly ship getting closer . . .
The waves getting higher, spitting and crashing.
There were boxes piled high on the greasy deck,
Damp from the salty spray of the sea.

The ship halted, I could hear the anchor hitting the seabed
Like someone was scraping their fingers along a chalkboard.
A beastly figure leaped off the deck
Hitting the wood with a high-pitched scratch.
I caught a glimpse of the creature's face,
Its bloodstained teeth, moulting fur and its eyes . . .
Its eyes were like stone,
So cold with a glint of burnt amber like leaves in autumn.
I watched the figure as it faded into the night,
I longed for answers.
I waited and waited but no one came.
The ship stood in the dark, rippled water,
Waiting for something,
Not a sound, not a voice, just deadly silence . . .

Heather Gray (13)
High School of Dundee, Dundee

The Sounds Of Fear

Hear the sound of night-time,
The rustling of the trees,
Drip, drip from the bathroom tap,
Whispers in the breeze.

Hear the sound of creaking,
The *slam!* of the front door,
A distant sound of tiptoes,
Echo on the floor.

Hear the sound of footsteps,
Coming up the stairs,
Pitter-patter, pitter-patter,
The noises come in pairs.

Hear the sudden *thump!*
Moving through the hall,
Floorboards creak, mice squeak,
But *I'm* not scared at all . . .

See the scary shadows,
Through the small gap in my door,
Can't see what it is,
But for legs - it's got four!

Hear the sound of thudding,
My heart's running a race,
The shadow is getting closer,
I can almost see its face . . .

Hear the sound of pouncing,
Right onto my bed!
Feel the touch of fur,
Covering its head!

Hear the sound of purring,
Because here in bed I'm sat,
Cuddling the 'monster' -
'Cause it's actually just my *cat!*

Charlotte Keatch (12)
High School of Dundee, Dundee

The Death Ship

As I hovered by the shore
Watching dogs and children play
I noticed a black silhouette on a new-blood horizon
It was a ship making bay
It drew in slowly
Sails roaring as if it had fought a mighty battle with the waves

As this ship drew closer, I noticed something
This ship was no medallious warrior
Those sails were without a roar
There was something missing, a crew

Sails and masts like skeletons
Snapping and whining as the wind nudged them
Sails not white with bravery but black with death and darkness
Wind whistled through cracks as if waking up ghosts and phantoms
As if crying out an arrival

This monster continued to lure towards me
The ocean began to look red
I clenched my eyes tight shut. The ship was too close.
Then I dared a peek
A rattling breath crept upon me
Whispering
Hissing

I turned to be pressed against a figure
It gently felt my hair and whispered in my ear
Then I looked at him
Eyes red with the blood the ship had sailed
I gazed longingly
Then that was the end.

Vanita Nathwani (13)
High School of Dundee, Dundee

The Hour When The Werewolves Howl

When the moon is bright and full,
When outside your hear a growl,
When you hear the drop of drool,
That's the hour when the werewolves howl.

When the world around you is dark,
When you see the shadows prowl,
When dogs are afraid to bark,
That's the hour when the werewolves howl.

When you see the blood-red eyes,
When you smell their breath so foul,
When you hear the children's cries,
That's the hour when the werewolves howl.

When you feel your blood run cold,
When you try but cannot yowl,
When things start to unfold,
That's the hour when the werewolves howl.

Lynsey Brown (12)
High School of Dundee, Dundee

The Hour When The Vampires Bite!

When the sky is as black as ink,
And the moon casts a silvery light,
When the wind whispers to the trees,
That's the hour when the vampires bite.

When the wolves howl in the darkness,
And an owl glides silently through the night,
When the bat forms an eerie silhouette in the sky,
That's the hour when the vampires bite.

When you hear a chilling cry,
And you awake from your dreams with a fright,
When you hear footsteps in the gloom,
That's the hour when the vampires bite.

When the colour drains from your face,
And you turn a ghostly white,
When a shiver goes down your spine,
That's the hour when the vampires bite.

Anna Mackenzie (11)
High School of Dundee, Dundee

The Hour When Demons Rage

When the cats and bats
Are round and about
And skulking in the dark
That's the hour when demons rage.

When the trees shake
And lightning crashes
And windows break
That's the hour when demons rage.

When the Devil laughs
And the witches fly
And children all cry and cry
That's the hour when demons rage.

When my hands are shaking
And my heart has stopped
And my voice is a whisper
That's the hour when . . .
Demons rage.

Kirsty Mitchell (12)
High School of Dundee, Dundee

The Dark Hates Me!

I think the dark hates me
Don't you?
It magnifies every grunt, shunt
Moan, groan, plip, plop, drip, drop
Bash, crash, squeak, creak
And even the tiniest bleep.

It turns your best friend into your worst enemy
Your comforts to your dreads
It holds a terrifying mask over everything it touches
Turning your favourite dreams to your nightmares.

It makes you question every quiver
Investigate every bang
With every squeak you shiver
And dread every clang.

It turns an artist's picture
To a spooky tree's bark
Every wonderful story
To deep, deathly dark.

Tristan Leicester (12)
High School of Dundee, Dundee

The Dark Forest

Deep down in the dark forest,
Shadows fell upon the green city,
Ferns swayed, foxes howled
And falcons cawed.
The trickling steam flowed down
The winding lane,
Foxgloves bent down
Like old men over the bubbling brook.

Ghastly ghosts glide between the
Tall trees,
Pale and peculiar,
Their silvery faces glow menacingly
In the moonlight.
Their presence is felt
But not seen.

The mist begins to rise
Up the terrifying tree's trunk.
The chaffinches chirp,
The ghosts grumble and
Crawl back to their shadowy places.

Rebecca Reid (11)
High School of Dundee, Dundee

Night-Time Stroll

Whispering, whistling and whining
The wind wails in the woods
The moon glistening pearly and white
My footsteps crunching the silvery snow
Rustle and ruffle the leaves.

And an eerie murmur as the cold wind bites
The graveyard glows in the gloom of the moon
The rotting corpses creak in their coffins
Deep, deep down beneath the surface of the earth.

The moans and the groans and the shrieks of pain
Echo through the cemetery
As the souls awaken and release their sorrow
A piercing scream as an owl howls in the night
Breaking the silence, making me shiver.

I hurry on, not wanting to linger
Sprinting and scurrying from this dead, dreary land
I never look back until I'm safe, clean away
Rid of my fears and hidden back home.

Siobhan Chien (11)
High School of Dundee, Dundee

Making Sense

Sometimes if it's really eerie you can hear them
Creaking, rustling, scratching
Then whispering, whistling and whining
But I'm told it is only me that can hear them.

Sometimes if you're on your own you can see them
Shuffling, dancing, devouring
Then roaming, running and raging
But I'm told it is only me that can see them.

Sometimes if you're really hungry you can taste them
Bitter sweet, tangy
Sickly, sour but succulent
But I'm told it is only me that can taste them.

Sometimes if it's dark they will touch me
Choking, scratching, scraping
Then poking, prodding and pinching
But I'm told it is only me that can feel them.

Sometimes in the dead of night you can smell them
Putrid, horrid, sickly
A smelly, stinking stench
But I'm told it is only me that can smell them.

Everyone says they don't exist
But I know they do
If you doubt me try using your senses tonight
You'll see, trust me, you will.

Alistair Lynch (12)
High School of Dundee, Dundee

The Lift

There was a crash
Then a thud
The lift went black
A shriek, 'Help!'
I heard a whisper
Then a moan
The lift door opened but not at my stop
Then a gruff voice: what was it saying?
The room, where was I?
What was that noise?
Oh, it was a deathly silence
A shuffle, a rustle
A thump and a bump
'Help!' I shouted again
I tried to run but fell onto the cold, hard floor
What was that? A crunch and a click
I scrambled up. What shall I do?
I looked up, a light beamed down
As I looked around all I saw were bones
I ran but there was no way out
The lift had gone
The wall of bones
They were closing in
'Help!' I shrieked again
No one came
I was doomed . . .

Freya Drummond (11)
High School of Dundee, Dundee

The Hour When The Ghosts Are Awake!

Screams can be heard all over the city,
The most haunted place in town is the lake,
All the parents show their children pity,
That's the hour when the ghosts are awake!

The blood oozed down the drain,
It came from the boy who had been stabbed by a rake,
The poor lad had suffered a lot of pain,
That's the hour when the ghosts are awake!

The sun had gone down, the moon was bright,
All those children who thought ghosts were fake,
They didn't know they would disappear in the night,
That's the hour when the ghosts are awake!

When all those children didn't return,
Their parents thought it must be a mistake,
Those unfortunate families need to learn,
That's the hour when the ghosts are awake!

Harry Ogilvie (12)
High School of Dundee, Dundee

The Hour When The Spirits Come

When the cold wind blows through the trees,
When the misty moon takes place of the sun,
When inky-black darkness is all you can see,
That's the hour when the spirits come.

When the huge owl's eyes watch for prey,
When cold rain against the window drums,
When scared creatures are crouched away,
That's the hour when the spirits come.

When loud screams are playing in your head,
When you wish you could cling to your mum,
When people start walking who used to be dead,
That's the hour when the spirits come.

When darkness is pressing in like snapping hounds,
When the presence of others makes you go numb,
When you hear eerie and terrifying sounds,
That's the hour when the spirits come.

Madeleine Adamson (12)
High School of Dundee, Dundee

My Hallowe'en Poem

When the temperature drops like a stone
When blood is chilled to the bone
When a storm ravages the sky
That's the hour when the zombies rise

When the night animals pause and listen
When eyes lose their glisten
When everything is as dark as the night
That's the hour when the zombies rise

When nice dreams come to a close
When you hear the moans and groans
When you begin to despise your life
That's the hour when the zombies rise

When the earth trembles with fear
When everyone is in tears
When the green, rotting hands extend from the depths of Hell
Now's the hour when the zombies rise.

David Bruce (12)
High School of Dundee, Dundee

Hallowe'en

Those glowing eyes looking at me
Those piercing eyes seem to look right through me
Those slanted eyes are shaped so perfectly
Oh, I hate those staring eyes

That twisted mouth with almost nothing inside
That sneering mouth that looks almost carved
That thin mouth that makes no noise,
Not even hiss, whine or bang
Oh, I hate that gaping mouth

That pointed nose with not one freckle on it
That long nose that doesn't seem to contain any nostrils
That orange-coloured nose that seems to be very flat
Oh, I hate that horrible nose

That misshaped face with such scary features
That strange face that seems hollow
That round face that is entirely orange
Oh, I really, really hate *pumpkins.*

Suzie Brown (11)
High School of Dundee, Dundee

The Ship Of Death

An old man lay upon his bed
Knowing that he would soon be dead
As night fell the dead ship set sail
And so began this eerie tale

Church bells struck the midnight hour
The moon sent down its ghostly glower
The man got up from his bed
And crossing to the window saw the ship of the dead

With a splintered mast and a ragged sail
The sight turned the old man pale
And as he saw its dark silhouette
Evil laughter rang out and the waves turned red

And at the helm of this vessel of death
Was a skeletal figure without a breath
While the figurehead with its silver scythe
Would constantly scream and howl and writhe

The ship came close and the old man went pale
For into his house the ship would sail
But when it collided neither broke
And the ship disappeared without a sound spoke

When they came next day to the old man's bed
They found him lying dead
But the expression on his face
Bore no fear, not even a trace.

Alistair Bell (13)
High School of Dundee, Dundee

A Ship Of Death

A ship on the horizon
A ship of seven ripped sails making the horizon look ragged
A ship that brought death
A ship that sails on the Devil's breath
This ship was sailing on the horizon.

A ship that is forever growing closer
A ship that is skeletal with jutting corpse bones
A ship with many guns ready to fire
A ship with a crew that do not tire
This ship was forever getting closer.

A ship that was nearing the land
A ship that sailed on gurgling blood
A ship that sails on winds that are like knives slashing the skin
A ship that fights enemies that never win
This ship was nearing the land.

A ship with its nose on the shore
A ship with a crew that is neither live nor dead
A ship that crashes and creaks and groans
A ship that is viciously pulled up on the stones
This ship has reached the land
And with it coming the sound of escaping footsteps.

Ewain Black (14)
High School of Dundee, Dundee

The Calling Of Death

The waves crashed up to me,
The bitter night nipped at my cheeks,
On the horizon a silhouette appeared,
A seeping, shaggy ship approaching the battered harbour,
Death drew closer, ever closer.

We were walking, drifting,
Alongside the demons,
Our worst nightmare looming in the storm,
As silent as the deep of night,
Death drew closer, ever closer.

The harbour crept into view,
The innocent arms of shelter,
Silently shrieking words of terror,
The ship slipped stealthily into the bay,
Death had arrived, it was here.

Kirsty Kilpatrick (13)
High School of Dundee, Dundee

The Dance

I see happy people dancing in clothes of red and pink
I see the calm, blue sea lapping against the pier
I hear the hungry seagulls greedily squawking for food
I hear the lapping sea splashing rocks nearby
I smell the salty sea
I smell food from a café I have not been to
I touch the boat which sways in the sea
I touch the wooden barriers saving us from falling
I taste food I've never tried before
I taste the finest of drinks
I feel hot with the sun so high in the sky
I feel like joining in this exotic dance.

Rachel Benson (13)
Invergordon Academy, Invergordon

Highland's Beauty

I see the grey sky looking like a schoolboy's jumper.
I see the sea reflecting the sky like a mirror.
I see houses crowded like London on Christmas Eve.
I see Kessock Bridge watching over the city
Like a mother watching her children.

I hear car engines like a Derby race.
I hear sheep bleating like Little Bo Peep's lost sheep.
I hear football fans ferociously roaring like a pack of hungry lions.
I hear the echoing noise of the waves crashing against the rocks.

I smell the fresh air flowing through my nostrils.
I smell the salty sea.
I smell the smoke coming from chimneys
As if I was standing in a burning building.
I smell fumes from all the traffic as if I was trapped in the exhaust.

I feel the wind blowing through my hair on this windy day.
I feel drops of rain on my bare arms.
I feel cold. Shivers run up my spine.
I feel lonely but with so many people near me
Like a candle without its flame.

Donna Dunn (13)
Invergordon Academy, Invergordon

All In A Night's Work

Before the guest house in Edinburgh,
They worked secretly for universities.
These men laboured only at night,
With shovels and bags.
Their sinister job soon ended when others joined in.
Together with their wives
They played host to many unsuspecting visitors.
A love of whisky then equalled a deadly night.

Tara Docherty (16)
Invergordon Academy, Invergordon

In The Fridge

I see
The rosy-red strawberries
The marmalade gleaming like the sun
The juicy, ripe tomatoes like Rudolph's nose

I hear
The food shouting out to me, 'Eat me, eat me,'
The rumble of my stomach as I see all the sights
The sound of my stomach telling my brain to eat
Over and over again like a broken record

I smell
The sweet, pleasant sniff of fresh fruits
The aroma of rich wine as I open the door
The whiff of cheese which slaps me like a smelly, old sock

I feel
The cold air surrounding me like a blanket
The hunger eating me up inside
The potent sting of onions like a needle in my eye

I taste
The sweet, juicy strawberries as I help myself
The smooth orange juice trickling down my throat
Like a gentle waterfall.

Tanya Calder (12)
Invergordon Academy, Invergordon

Forgiven

I see stars.
There is only one that defines me.
Shadows attack in numbers
Along with symbols of their own.
A close friend once told me,
'We have lived in fear, now we can live in hope.'
I still believe, in spite of everything,
That people are good at heart.

Jordan Mitchell (16)
Invergordon Academy, Invergordon

Utopia

I see a cloudless, blue sky, as blue as a cornflower.
    A majestic, rocky mountain, watching over everything.
    Emerald-green grass, lush and welcoming.
    Two mares, tranquil and at peace.

I hear birds full of life, singing and chirruping.
    Leaves rustling as a gentle breeze blows through them.
    The soft nickering of the horses, content just to graze.

I smell newly-mown grass, sweet and refreshing.
    Home cooking, cakes and bread, wafting through my nostrils.
    Pollen, making me sneeze as I laugh in delight.

I taste the fruits in the orchard, mouth-watering and delicious.
    The ham sandwich I packed, succulent and tasty.
    A honeyed sensation of freedom.

I touch the stubs of shorn grass, damp beneath my fingertips.
    The sky with outstretched hands, near, yet so far away.
    The wind and the sun and everything around me,
    Breathing as one.

I feel as if I am in an unknown paradise.
    The earth is in harmony with every being.
    The world is my oyster.

Emily Goodwin (13)
Invergordon Academy, Invergordon

The Artist's Ending

The artist stands back,
Admiring his work.
His creation is a canvas of vivid, bright colours.
The masterpiece glows like a fiery dragon,
Prowling the August sky after the kill.
He peers cautiously over the mushroom,
Such a contrast of emotions.
This monstrosity has destroyed man,
So more may live.

Daniel Hogarth (16)
Invergordon Academy, Invergordon

Feelings Of A Hunted Snowboarder

I see a helicopter following me
Like a missile with an attached sniper rifle
Being controlled by the enemy.

I hear the propellers swirling above my head
With a mission to kill.

I smell my own fear as I know I am not going to escape from this
But I won't give up.

I feel the fresh air as I fly off the cliff
In my last attempt to avoid death.

I taste my heart as it comes into my mouth
For the first time in my career
Then I taste the snow as I hit the ground.

Thomas Baird (13)
Invergordon Academy, Invergordon

The Race Of A Lifetime

I see the gates open
I thunder past the blurred crowd
I see all the other horses as I fly past them

I hear the crowd roaring like lions
I hear whips like a flock of birds flapping their wings

I smell the burgers as I fly past the crowd
I taste the flies as I accidentally swallow them

I touch the horse's mane as soft as silk
I pat him on the neck as we cross the finish line

I slowly pull on the reins

I feel as happy as a dog with a bone
As a winner waiting for his trophy

Suddenly I hear all the other horses
Thunder past the finish line.

Kerry Armstrong (12)
Invergordon Academy, Invergordon

Palm Trees

I see big palm trees like umbrellas
I see some clouds like white smoke moving in the wind
I see a girl like Angelina Jolie

I hear the palm trees like acorns falling
I hear the girl humming like a bird

I smell the girl like a rose
I smell the sand like a fish

I taste the salty sea

I touch the tree, wrinkly like Grandma
I touch the smooth skin of the sexy lady

I feel happy as I am beside the lady and the sea!

Sean Sutherland (13)
Invergordon Academy, Invergordon

Simply Supple

The crowds shuffle like a flock of penguins,
Many amongst them whisper quieter
Than a gentle breeze.
Soft crunches of feet fill the gym
Like echoes in a cave.

The strong aroma of sweat fills my
Nose like a stuffy cold.
My face is as stiff as a board
With all the stress.

I can taste nothing but fear,
If I mess up I will ruin my reputation.

The squidgy touch of mats
Soothes my hands.
I truly feel bendier than
A tree in a hurricane.

Sarah Sinclair (13)
Invergordon Academy, Invergordon

Icy Fun

I see
Someone falling as heavily as a load of bricks
Lying on the ice like Bambi falling
Sitting on the ice like a plant in the ground
Smiling like a Cheshire cat

I hear
Laughing as loud as in a late-night club
Shouting as deafening as a disco
Thuds like a baby elephant
Scraping like the rasp of a file

I taste
Air as icy as a freezer
Air as cold as a snowy, winter's day
Air that's fresh like water on the hill
Freshness like her toothpaste

I touch
Ice that's rough like sandpaper
Ice that's chilly like a frosty morning
Ice as sharp as a piece of glass
Wetness like having a bath

I feel
As frozen as an ice lolly
As miserable as coming last in a race
As determined as a lion after a zebra
As sad as a pig going to market.

Wendy Brown (12)
Invergordon Academy, Invergordon

Along Rainbow Street

Sauntering along Rainbow Street
I see the colourful surroundings
Signposts, cars, buildings
And people create the technicolor mayhem
As bright and wild as an explosion in a paint factory

Walking along Rainbow Street
I hear the busy and rushed sounds of the city
People yelling and vehicles zooming from the crowds of disruption
As varied in loud sounds as a music festival

Wandering along Rainbow Street
I smell the disgusting mixture of local scents
The takeaway, petrol fumes
And floods of people
As different in smells as a chef's kitchen

Drifting along Rainbow Street
I taste the delicious food that I eat
Local cuisine of fried rice and green tea
Make the tasty combination
As exquisite as the country in which they are made

Strutting along Rainbow Street
I touch the things which are close to me
My warm dish of rice and the hot cup of tea I clasp in my hands
As comforting as light in the dark

Sauntering along Rainbow Street
The sight of the busy town and the sound of the mayhem
The scents that are around me and the taste of the food
I feel at home
I know that I'm in Rainbow Street.

Rachael Bews (13)
Invergordon Academy, Invergordon

Summer Fridge

I see
Shelves of blue,
Red tomatoes too.
Soft orange juice,
As cool as the colour blue.

I hear
My stomach rumbling,
As I see all of the
Wonderful food in
Front of me.

I smell
The fresh pasta,
Like newly-picked
Flowers on a
Summer's day.

I taste
The juicy, red
Strawberries,
They melt in my mouth
Like ice cream.

I touch
The funny-shaped egg,
That nearly falls out of my hand.

I feel
A cold shiver up my spine,
Like a cold kangaroo.
I quickly close the fridge.

Mairi M MacLeod (13)
Invergordon Academy, Invergordon

Taken

I see soldiers as
Tough as nails
I see the sun
As bright as
A thousand candles
I see tears running down my face
Like an overflowing river

I hear screeching
Like owls in the night
I hear the heavy footsteps
Of the officers as loud as
Elephants stamping
I hear men groaning
Like caged lions

I smell the sweat of soldiers
Like being in a rugby players'
Changing room
I smell gunpowder as horrid as
Rotting cabbage

I taste the dirt from the struggle
Like acid in my mouth
I taste my tears like sweet sugar
I taste the air as polluted as the
Barrel of toxic waste

I touch the arm of my captor as
Strong as an angered gorilla
I touch the rough suit as coarse as
A horse's mane
I touch the armoured belts
Like thorns in my side

I feel the hot air on my feet
Like placing them in a furnace
I feel as alone as a
Wolf howling in the night
I feel betrayed by friends who broke
A strong trust.

Amy Bremner (13)
Invergordon Academy, Invergordon

Wreckage

I see destruction, the ruined bus lying in the road,
I see seats that have been flung from the bus
Like stones from a catapult,
I see devastation beyond the wreckage of a Hollywood film.

I hear screaming like a pig on a fire,
I hear the cries of children like hungry babies,
I hear ripping metal like the buckling of a boat's hull.

I smell raw metal like steel from a factory,
I smell the acrid burning like a bomb just gone off,
I smell traffic fumes from a busy London street.

I touch the ice-cold metal like the polished surface of an ice rink,
I touch the broken glass from the shattered windows,
I touch the razor-sharp metal like the edge of a circular saw.

I feel horrified, like seeing someone murdered before my eyes,
I feel sickened at the sight of such wreckage,
I feel scared thinking that we think we are safe.

Liam Irvine (13)
Invergordon Academy, Invergordon

Outdoors

I see the grass that's green as emeralds
I see a fence like Connect 4
I see the deep red cutters that are like roses

I hear the wind whistling as if it was happy
I hear the snaps of the cutters like crocodiles crunching
I hear the wire tapping a tune on the fence

I smell the air as cold as a freezer
I smell the grass like perfume
I smell the wood like being in a woodwork room

I taste the cold air in my mouth like an ice cream
I taste the plants like a greenhouse in my mouth

I touch the smooth cutters that feel like a baby's skin
I touch the wire like a blunt knife
I touch the uneven wood that's sharp like the edges of a fireplace

I feel the soft fabric like a blanket covering me
I feel the wire dig into me like a doctor taking my blood pressure
I feel the wind slapping my face.

Rachel Michael (13)
Invergordon Academy, Invergordon

The Race

I see the blurred colours of the
Audience as I race past.
I see my speed dial slowly creep
Up as I turn into a straight.
They see me as I speed past an
Opponent.
They see me tear away from the
Pack as the race begins.

I hear my supporters roar like
A pack of hungry lions.
I hear my engine rumbling like
A stampede of buffalo.
They hear the screeching sound
Of rubber on tarmac.

I taste the anticipation of the
Fans in the stadium.
I can taste the greasy burgers
That the fans are eating.
They taste the excitement that
Is thick through the air.

I feel the engine purring as
I start the car.
I feel the butterflies fluttering
In my stomach.
They feel the thrill as cars
Reach alarming speeds.

I touch the hearts of many people
As I pass the finish line.
I touch the leather steering wheel
As its surface grips my fingertips.
They touch each other in celebration
As I win!

Dean Thomson (13)
Invergordon Academy, Invergordon

Forest Ride

I see the forest ahead of me
In all its glory.
I hear woodland noises and
The crackle of the twigs and leaves
Under my tyre
Like the sound of a fire.
I smell the coldness of the
Air like daggers to my nose.
I taste the mist in the air
As I breathe it in.
I touch the cold grip of
The handlebars.
I see a great, huge oak tree
As I zoom past.
I hear the sound of little
Woodland animals scurrying
Into the leaves like scrunched
Up newspaper.
I smell wet wood
Like a wet dog.
I taste the hot, milky taste of
The cup of tea, which awaits me.
I touch the cold mud that has
Splattered me like water to a car
In a car wash.
I see a squirrel in a tree
Like a statue.
I hear the wind whistling
In my ears.
I smell the rich aroma of ferns.
I taste the sugary taste of a
Glucose sweet that gives me energy.
I touch the hard metal lever of
The back brake as I skid around
The corner.

    I feel great!

Alasdair Turner (13)
Invergordon Academy, Invergordon

My Favourite Time Of Year

I see children scuttling about ecstatically.
I hear the crunch of snow as Dad walks up the path.
I smell the aroma of chocolate muffins baking in the oven.
I taste the freezing cold, razor-sharp ice of a snowball.
I touch the freezing unevenness of the snow.
I feel warm, fuzzy and relaxed despite the cold.

I see Dad getting pounded with snowballs
As he struggles to get to the car door.
I hear the laughter of children having fun.
I smell the exhaust fumes from the car.
I taste the delicious muffins Mum has made.
I touch the cold glass pane on the window.
I feel the joy of the time of year.

I see a girl run around the car.
I hear Dad honking the car horn.
I smell the perfume of my sister.
I taste the bacon sandwich I made.
I touch the cold brass door handle.
I feel the need to pulverise Dad as he steps out the car door.

Robert Michael (13)
Invergordon Academy, Invergordon

Jerry's Café

I see a man
With an elegant, up-to-date jacket
Which looked like weak tea.
I see a sign,
As black as the dark night
With writing as white as a sheepskin.

I hear the sound of the door
Pound as it opens and closes.
I hear the people
Chatting like old hens.

I smell the aroma
Of the indulgent coffee from
The steam as it bounces off my face.
I smell the pollution
From the cars as they race past the café.

I taste the coffee
As it runs down my throat.
I taste the morning fry-up
Sizzling in the pan.

I touch the smooth, leather chair
Like a glossy magazine.
I touch the rough, cloudy table
Like tiny, little stones.

I feel revived
Like a baby wakening up
From its afternoon sleep.
I feel lonely
Like a dog without his bone.

Carly Yeaman (13)
Invergordon Academy, Invergordon

Elegance

I see an elegant woman
Standing as tall as a tower
Her gleaming diamond jewellery
Shines into the light like stars.

I hear her jewellery
Clanking like metal
Her high heels
Crisply hit the floor like cymbals.

I smell her cigar
Puffing scented smoke like a burning oven
Her newly applied perfume
Like a fresh summer's day.

I taste the pink champagne
That tickles my throat like a feather
The strawberries that
Are as sweet as candy.

I touch the black material
Of her dress like a cat's fur
Her jewellery as
Cool as ice.

I feel the smoke from her cigar soar
Through my fingers like a soft breeze.
I feel the ground shake as she walks
Making the ground quiver like an earth tremor.

Lynn Semple (12)
Invergordon Academy, Invergordon

Food, Glorious Food

I see the golden garlic bread
As bright as the sun
I see a graceful flower
As it sits up elegantly.

I hear the butter
As it is scraped along the toasted bread
I hear the shake of a sieve
Like the rattle on the end of a snake.

I smell the golden butter
As it melts into the garlic bread
I smell the fragrant flower
As fresh as a summer's morning.

I taste the garlicky bread
As it slowly dissolves down my throat
I taste the sweet icing flower
As it melts on my tongue
Like butter melting in a frying pan.

I touch the crispy crust
Like a dried up leaf
I touch the smooth petals
As the freshly-mixed icing is squeezed upon it.

I feel the heat from the bread
Like the warmth from a radiator
I feel the icing sugar fall from the sieve
As it slips through my fingers.

Jasmin Ross (13)
Invergordon Academy, Invergordon

Smoking Kills

I see a long-term smoker's hands
With nicotine stains by the finger
Nails holding the deadly weapon that
Caused this damage.
I hear the deep, dirty breath taken
Causing the lungs to turn to tar.
I smell the disgusting reek of smoke
That is choking me.
I taste the smoke that is crawling
Down my throat.
I feel choked.
I can't believe
That someone would abuse their
Body
Like this.

Erin Robson (13)
Invergordon Academy, Invergordon

Winter

The mornings are as dark as night,
Ice lies peacefully on the car windows,
Frost rests quietly over a sea of grass until
The morning sun melts it slowly.

It brightens up as the morning goes by
You walk across the grass,
Any frost left crunches under your feet as
If it weren't there.

The first drops of snow fall to the ground,
Its minding its own business and it finds a place to sit,
It falls all around all day,
This is the start of winter!

Diane Whittle (15)
Kelso High School, Kelso

Orca

The orca is a huge and friendly mammal
Although well known as the killer whale,
It is no beast or killer,
It is intelligent,
It is noisy,
And athletic,
As it leaps through the waves of the harsh sea.

The orca is mostly black,
With a few white patches,
And small black eyes,
Its fins are small,
But the dorsal is rather tall,
And the tail fins are wide,
The orca is no killer,
It is a friendly giant,
Who means or brings no harm.

Stephanie Cockburn (14)
Kelso High School, Kelso

The Great War

Fix the barbed wire; that's just one chore,
Please don't give me anymore
My feet are *so* sore.
I hate this stench,
When are we ever getting out of this trench?
At Christmas we sang,
It's now replaced with a bang.
Our last tank eaten by mud,
Our only food stolen by the flood.
How many soldiers hurt?
A two minute silence ruined by one blurt.

Carrie Jardine (15)
Kelso High School, Kelso

Battle

The battle commences
Two sides both fighting for freedom
They bring out their cannons
Bang!
Boom!
They charge
Both sides clash

Swords swinging
Spears clashing
Blood everywhere, dead bodies on the ground
One side starts their cannons again
Boom!
It hits a score of men

The battle still goes on
Everyone hitting and stabbing each other
Neither side's breaking down
They are still hacking at each other
But now the archers release a shower of arrows hitting everywhere

Now the lines are destroyed
Everyone who survived is now backing down
They retreat
They run to their castle.

Craig Watson (13)
Kelso High School, Kelso

Wicked Car

Citroen Saxo VTR
Wicked engine, wicked car
Body kit, neon light,
Two-tone paint - what a sight!
Twin exhaust, induction kit,
Bucket seats for you to sit,
Tank of NOS will do the job
McNero's on the rob.

Jamie Mitchell (15)
Kelso High School, Kelso

Chocolate

Chocolate, so delicious
Whether it's smooth milk chocolate,
Or a crunchy Belgian chocolate,
So delicious.

Chocolate, so delicious
Biting into the advanced version of the rich cocoa bean
All the way from Ecuador,
So delicious.

Chocolate, so delicious
Letting it melt away in your mouth,
Like an ice cream in the sun,
So delicious.

Chocolate, so delicious
You can't get enough of it,
Smooth, bubbly, crunchy, or chewy,
So delicious.

Chocolate, so delicious
Whatever type it is,
You can't beat it,
So delicious.

Phillip Hume (15)
Kelso High School, Kelso

Witty

When everything is said and done,
No one is a patch on me for fun,
The clever one, the witty one, the ideal man,
When I'm on my court, I play like no other can.
I'm too damn smooth for anyone,
No time for booze, sleep or food,
I hang around just being me,
The sexiest ever dude!

Paul Simpson (15)
Kelso High School, Kelso

Feelings

Cold, blue, a tear streams down my face
Silence, nothing
I feel hurt, I feel alone
Dark, empty
I curl up into a ball
I feel hurt, I feel alone

Warm, orange and jumpy
A grin from ear to ear
I feel happy, I feel joyful
Exuberant, bright
Laughing like a hyena
I feel happy, I feel joyful

Hot, red envy in my eyes.
Clenched fish, gritting teeth
I feel angry, I feel mad.
Bad thoughts run through my head
Fire, hate
I feel angry, I feel mad

The look in his eyes, the touch of his hands
Floating, dreaming
I feel love, I feel cherished
The scent of his cologne rushes through me and lifts me up
Pink, passionate
I feel love, I feel cherished.

Kerry Bell   (14)
Kelso High School, Kelso

A Thing Called Love

Everyone is talking, everyone is dancing.
He is listening to the band,
Taking in everything they say.
She is at the bar,
Watching him.
His dark hair is hanging over his perfect blue eyes.
She knows that he will never notice her,
Still she waits.
Her heart beats faster as he walks over.
She looks at him, but he doesn't see.
If only it was as simple as just going to talk to him,
But she doesn't know how.
She can smell his sweet scent after he swept by her.
He is sitting down.
Now is her chance, she just needs to get up and go over . . .
She freezes.
He is looking at her and she is looking at him.
Their eyes lock, and everything freezes.
She can feel her heart beating as fast as a puppy's tail.
The beats are getting louder and louder.
Her own nerves are suffocating her.
The butterflies in her stomach are out of control.
Suddenly it's over and he looks away.
He slowly gets up and walks over, but only to walk past her again.
It happened, it was true and she will never forget him.

Vicki Freshwater (14)
Kelso High School, Kelso

Golf

The wind blowing on my face
Makes you feel as cool as an ice cube.
The lush green grass blowing steadily in the breezy wind.
The sound of someone hitting the ball at you.
The shouting of *'Fore!'*
The proud look on your face when you have just bought shiny
                                                    new clubs.
The sound of the titanium club hitting the Calloway Z60 gold distance
                                                    golf ball.

As the fresh crisp smell of a summer's morning.
The musty smell of the autumn leaves rotting into the ground.
And the crisp, white grass of a winter morning.
A proud feeling rushes over your body when you shoot an eagle, a
                                                    birdie or a par.
The feeling of guilt when you shoot a bogie or a double bogie.
Then the relief of starting a fresh hole and a fresh score.
Then the anger of you shouting and swearing if you hit a bogie on
                                                    two holes in a row.
The shame when you blame your old equipment when you didn't
                                                    play well,
But you know inside that it is your own fault.
The apprehension of waiting to see if you have won the competition.
And the feeling of joy when you get awarded with a trophy when you
                                                    win it.

Steven Robson (14)
Kelso High School, Kelso

My Monster

My monster would be enormous so that everyone had to look up to it,
It would have a raging temper like a volcano about to erupt,
It would have a grin of mischief and fun,
And a laugh of evil,
It would have eyes so bright they would be enough to blind you,
But its heart would be made out of gold
Enough to share all round.

Amanda Charters (15)
Kelso High School, Kelso

Nobody's Child

She sits there all on her own,
Nobody cares.
Her capacious eyes stare out of the shadows,
Nobody cares.
None of the people walking past see her,
As nobody cares about nobody's child.

The bright lights and busy street seem miles away,
Nobody cares.
Her ribs stick out, her eyes are sunken,
Nobody cares.
Her ragged clothes hang off her skeletal substance,
Nobody cares about nobody's child.

Her glossy eyes reflect the street, the people, the life,
Nobody cares.
Her tears run down her face and hit the pavement below,
Nobody cares.
She curls up in a ball and slowly dies,
Nobody cares about nobody's child.

Katie Pettigrew (12)
Kelso High School, Kelso

The Spirit Of Christmas

Christmas the best time of the year
The cheery atmosphere
Build up of excitement
The wintry nights where children are playing in the snow
Then getting warmed up by the fire
The tree decorating and turkey roasting
Carol singers singing festive songs on your doorstep
Children not getting to sleep by wondering what Father Christmas
will bring

That's the spirit of Christmas.

Grant Charters (12)
Kelso High School, Kelso

Love

As I look into his eyes
He takes my breath away
His kiss so warm and tender
The touch of an angel

When I lie in his big, strong, warm arms
It feels as if nothing could take
This feeling of love from me

When he walks away from me
I feel empty inside
But when he returns my world is complete

His smile takes me away
Into our own little world
Which I never want to leave

The look in his eye tells me
He'll never leave me
The touch of his hand
Says he'll catch me
Wherever I fall

When I hear the words,
'I love you
I always will'
My heart stops as I reply,
'I will love your forever, our love will never end'

This man I love
I could never stop loving him
It seems he feels the same.

Our love is so strong . . .

Georgina Woodhead (14)
Kelso High School, Kelso

Civic Week

The feeling of a soft coat of fur.
The colours of the early morning as the sun rose.
It was time for pony club camp, 8.00am on a Monday morning.
That's when it starts.
The excitement of what horse you were taking
What group you will be in.
Firstly you would do the cross-country
The colour of the spooky jumps
The feeling of the wind in your face,
The sound of the horses panting.
That's cross-country.
Secondly you would do the six bar
The colour of the six jumps in a row
The feeling of the spring over the jump.
Tuesday the show-jumping starts
The colour of the colourful jumps and fillers.
Next up is the dressage
The sound of the thumping from the horses.
The last day of the pony club camp is the competition day
First up is the games
The sound of the cheering.
Second up, the prizes
The sound enjoyment.
Third up is saying bye to all your new friends.
Saturday morning the big ride out
The sound of loads of horses
The feeling of excitement and joy.
The sound of the horn to set off
Tat the end the feeling of sadness
The sight of the lorries driving away
Civic week is over.

Kayleigh Beveridge (14)
Kelso High School, Kelso

Slipping Away

Her salted tears smother the faces behind the transparent glass,
A man and a lady smile at her holding a glass of fizzing champagne,
She weeps as the people she once loved slip through her fingers,
Six years before,
Six feet under, surrounded by a wooden box,
Nothing but the cold damp air for company,
She is lonely, in despair, wondering the earth for one thing only,
The girl at the age of eight sitting in a bath,
Surrounded in bubbly froth like the champagne,
'Is Granny going to die? *Ring! Ring!* Granny is dead,'
Four and a half years on he sits and stares,
Using the phone as a link from loneliness,
A rare visit, a rare physical encounter with a human being,
The girl walked home from a night of laughs,
I bet Grandad is dead, she thinks out of the blue,
Carved into the marble stone another name appears with thin
                                                golden curves,
They say a heart attack but deep down it was loneliness,
The split that grew and grew mended as soon as the red blood
                                                stopped circulating,
The girl closed her eyes tight
Touched the gravestone that she couldn't visit,
Felt the engraving and the flowers at its feet,
A tear then escaped from a million and fell to the ground
                                                she imagined,
The patchwork seams once split and fell apart,
The patchwork of two broken hearts that thought it was all over,
Now the seams are sewn together forever like the love that will never
                                                die again,
The lady and the man sit together with a glass of fizzing champagne,
Goodnight for now but not forever.

Bryony Nisbet (14)
Kelso High School, Kelso

The Snow

The weather forecast predicted snow and lots of it,
I ran to the front door,
Put my wellies, gloves, hat, scarf and coat on,
And went to play in the snow,
It was like a white sheet tucked tightly on a bed,
The snow covered the ground,
No grass or stones could poke through,
Not even when you made a footprint,
You couldn't even touch the ground.

Looking around,
The icicles tinkled and the small snowflakes falling sparkled,
I was stunned at the snow kingdom,
Before I reached the garden gate another blizzard hit,
I couldn't see,
When it passed the snow was up to my knees,
It was lucky; there were steps to my door,
Rooftops were white,
Drifts were falling off the trees,
As I waded through the snow all I could hear was crunch . . . crunch.

Rolling a snowball in my hand,
It was cold and hard,
It was good for snowmen and angels
Delicate snowflakes fell onto my shoulders,
The snow had no smell,
Nor taste,
You could see the white sky,
Plenty of snow,
And the green off the fir trees was only showing under the branches,
Unfortunately I had to go in.

Robyn Hall (14)
Kelso High School, Kelso

Smile

Sometimes it seems like we're not meant to be happy and smiling
just isn't today,
It hits us all, some more than others and we just can't shake it away,
Piling up is negativity, leaving stacks of worries and thoughts
Drifting out is a hopeful mind that quite simply, positively taught
Take a deep breath, feel the air, watch the birds and hold a smile
You have to hold onto some little but precious moments to make
life worthwhile
Don't take for granted that you have been given whether good
or bad,
So try to listen to what I've said and make some happiness from
the sad,
One last thing, leave the past behind and look forward, not back,
don't dread
Just try your best; you soon will see the happiness has clearly spread.

Rachel Waters (15)
Kelso High School, Kelso

Grey

Everything's grey.
Behind grey bars and boxed up in grey walls.
In a grey straight suite.
Struggling, squirming to break free.
Bloodshot eyes and a bloody nose is plastered over my face.
I scream and shout
And realise there's not enough air to breath or scream.
Whatever I do or say makes no difference in this cell.
My dreams are of freedom.
Oh to be free!
But even my dreams are grey
I can't touch, can't feel, smell, taste or even hear.
But one day I shall break from this senseless cell and break free.
Till then I'll have to wait. But for how long?

Claire Page (15)
Kelso High School, Kelso

The Weather

The weather's cold for most of the year,
It makes you wonder,
Why couldn't we be in the southern hemisphere?
Why couldn't the weather be warm?

The weather's always cold and raining,
Blowing a gale, hail or something bad
And although I don't like complaining
Why couldn't it be warm?

The weather's always cold this time of year
It's always raining, cold
Or gales blowing in your ear.
Why couldn't it be warm?

The weather's cold day and night
It's always windy, freezing or raining
It's enough to give you a fright
Why couldn't it be warm?

The weather's really boring
It's always really similar,
It is usually raining or pouring
Why couldn't it be warm?

Steven Jeffrey (15)
Kelso High School, Kelso

The Storm

There was a terrible storm
The night the ship went down.
The waves were towering above us,
Crashing all around.
The rain was lashing against our faces,
The wind was howling in our ears.
We couldn't see for tuppence
And ended up crashing into the pier.

Calum Bruce (15)
Kelso High School, Kelso

Rainbow Warmer

The nose of a clown
The beat of a heart
The colour of anger
Red

The sweetness of an orange
The colour of calm
The pumpkin pie
Orange

The perfect sunshine
A daisy in the wind
Banana madness
Yellow

The crispy apple
Magical grass
The colour of fun
Green

The bottomless ocean
The endless sky
A colour of sadness
Blue

The girl's girl
Popular
Special
Indigo

Express yourself
Lose yourself
Swim in colour
Violet.

Rhona Anderson (15)
Kelso High School, Kelso

Exam

Sitting in a room;
Only four walls to hold me,
Everyone is silent -
The teacher comes in,
They talk,
But still everything is silent.
The phone rings, the teacher goes out.
The room is filled with laughter and joy until they return.
It is silent again.

The bell rings for break,
We leave in a group,
Go for break with that thought in our head -
Who is our next teacher?
Are they nice or are they not?
We don't know.
We go to our next class.
It is about our exams.
It is frightening.
I want to escape, but I can't.
They're stood there staring at me.
I want to scream.
My exams are so close, yet so far.
I know not to worry;
But it's too late -
I'm panicking,
I'm sweating,
I can't speak.
The teacher asks me a question on my exam.

I'm there.

Michelle Condy-Smith (15)
Kelso High School, Kelso

100 Metres

I wonder what it feels like to go that fast.
To feel like a bullet from a gun
As you explode out of the blocks,
To feel every muscle tense
In the first stride,
To feel like a cheetah
Tearing up the ground behind its prey,
To feel like the wind itself
Speeding up the track,
To feel like a racehorse
Stretching for the line,
To feel the agony
After the last demanding metres,
I wonder what it feels like to win the Olympic gold.

Andrew Hogarth (15)
Kelso High School, Kelso

Changing Images

It starts with long blonde curls and flapper skirts
But soon replaced by black hair and gothic coats
Then there are girly dresses and polka dots
Afterwards its skater shorts and stripy socks.

There's the rock chick with ripped jeans
Tomorrow she's a hippy in a tie-dye poncho
One minute she's a redhead in a gypsy top
Ten she's a brunette with her cowboy boots.

This is what fashion is all about
Dramatic changes and brand new looks
It's amazing how our image transforms
But do we look different or just the same?

Megan Wilde (15)
Kelso High School, Kelso

My Friend Has A Horse Called Star

My friend has a horse called Star
She doesn't live very far
She lives on a hill and stays very still
And doesn't move all day.

Star has a mum called Rolos
Her favourite food is Polos
Her colour is bay
And she loves to neigh.

Her saddle fits her
That's why I love her to bits.
Her coat is so warming
Especially in the frosty, cold morning.

Laura Mulvie (12)
Kelso High School, Kelso

Poppies

Silky, delicate petals
Glowing in the sunlight,
Flowing over the land like blood.

Long stems swaying in the breeze,
Backwards and forwards,
Falling like the wounded.

Dark centres drawing the eye,
Permanent and sinister,
Like holes left by bullets.

So vivid and colourful,
They demand attention,
Like the explosion of a shell.

Sarah Watson (15)
Kelso High School, Kelso

A Troublesome Thing

A poem is such a difficult thing to write,
And to rhyme,
You need to stay up all the night,
And spend a lot of time,
On finding words and phrases,
Searching here and there,
As Mum stands and gazes,
Your eyes turn square,
And you realise your pencil lead,
Has vanished, as has your paper,
Maybe you should just go to bed,
And finish your stupid poem later.

Katie Holmes-Smith (15)
Kelso High School, Kelso

Am I Invisible?

Am I invisible?
It's as if I'm not there
They look at me like they don't care
What have I done wrong?

Is it my eyes, face, body or shape?
Maybe it's the way I dress
I always try to look my best
What have I done to them?

It's them who point and laugh
All I want to happen is for me to fit in
Why can't they have some discipline?
Will they ever show me respect?

Sarah Strathdee (13)
Kelso High School, Kelso

Am I The Only One Here?

I licked up every crumb from my plate
Then grabbed my coat without any care
I ran to school thinking I would be late
Managed to enter the grounds with a minute to spare.

The main door was locked to my dislike
So I detoured to the small door round the other side,
Oh, how I wished I had brought my bike!
Something was different, the rush of people like a strong
                                              flowing tide.

It wasn't there!

I pressed the door open with eagerness
And I entered the big empty hall
I wondered, *where are all the rest?*
All that was in sight was an abandoned gym ball.

I decided to see if anyone was in class
I started my journey to the other end of the school
Where are my classmates, the loud, rambling mass?
Then it struck me, oh what a fool!
It's a Saturday, there is no school!

Jenna Simpson (13)
Kelso High School, Kelso

The Hills

This lifeless landscape never changes,
Nor does the sound from the babbling brook,
Or the endless mew of the buzzard somewhere in the distance.

As the sun sets over this enchanted land,
The many shades of green and brown are hidden for another day.

Rachel Butler (13)
Kelso High School, Kelso

Life's Such A Mess

Your life's a mess,
Because no one likes you,
Not even your parents.
So there's no one there
For you.
When you need them.
No one talks
To you at home.
You get bullied
By Julie the bully.
But tell me
What have I done
To them
For them to not like me?
I have been watching
Too much of 'The Bill'
and want to kill
myself. And things
Will be better
For everyone.
So I say goodbye
To my mum, dad
And they don't
Even care
They just need
Some air and
Get over it.

Lesley Chaman (13)
Kelso High School, Kelso

Winter

The ice was cold
The ice was slippy
It was a hazard on the way to the chippy
I slipped and fell on my back
I could hear my neck crack
I went home, I felt alright
But I ended up in hospital that night
In the morning at half-eight
I felt great
I went outside and what a state
The world was black
I went outside and I heard a crack
It was my back
The ice was cold
The ice was slippy . . .

David Sanderson (13)
Kelso High School, Kelso

Christmas Time

Christmas is the best
Time of the year.
But after it's all over
It brings a tear.
All the presents that I get
Are mainly chocolate.
When Santa comes on his sleigh
With his reindeer hip, hip hooray!
Presents big, present small
And some are very, very tall.

Jamie Noble (13)
Kelso High School, Kelso

Hallowe'en

Owls hoot in the woods as I walk by,
The trees sway to and fro in the wind,
A bright moon shines high above me.
It's dark, the air is so calm and quiet,
I feel scared in the woods alone.

A white mist stands in front of me,
I let out a scream. It vanishes.
Was it a ghost?

It's silent again, I see a person in a black coat,
Blood dripping from its face.
I jump back in fright. It dashes off.
Was it a vampire?

I run out of the woods, like a bullet from a gun
I come to a busy street,
Children are trick or treating, you can smell the hot toffee apples
I go home; a glowing pumpkin welcomes me,
This is the Hallowe'en I know.

Ashley Fairbairn (14)
Kelso High School, Kelso

Christmas

I looked out the window on Christmas morning
Then went to get my family
We went down the stairs and opened the door
And through it you could see the Christmas tree

We opened our presents one at a time
And then went through for some lovely food
We had eggs, bacon and a cup of tea
I was ever so happy!

Tanyta Johnston (13)
Kelso High School, Kelso

American Football

It's the sight of thousands of fans
And the roar when there's a touchdown
You feel really good
When one of the players
From the team that you're against gets nailed
The smell of the food going round the whole stadium
How nervous you feel before the game,
When the team that's against you
Gets close to the touchline
How good you feel
When your team wins
How annoyed you are
When they lose.

Shaun McNulty (14)
Kelso High School, Kelso

Life

Life ebbs and flows,
Before you know it you're in a home,
You're born and your parents are very happy.
Next minute you're eighteen and leaving the home.
You go and get a job
Next minute you're retired.
You have a wife and you have kids,
Next minute your kids have left the home and you're now
                                        a grandparent.

Life ebbs and flows
Before you know it you're in a home
It's a matter of time.

Callum Patterson (12)
Kelso High School, Kelso

Christmas Day

'Sssh!' The children slowly tiptoed down the stairs.
As they went into the living room
Their eyes lit up
There were so many presents under the tree
They were so excited to open them
Mum and Dad came down the stairs
One by one they opened the presents.
Rustle! Goes the paper as it's chucked on the floor
As their presents started to fade so did their smiles
The Christmas tree glistened
The tinsel sparkled
The fairy on the top of the tree looked down on the whole family
Smells of turkey, potatoes and gravy were coming from the kitchen
Gradually the family flowed through the front door
Kissing and hugging
More presents were opened
More thank yous were said
Finally the dinner was cooked
Everyone sat down
They all dug in, passing things round the table
Soon everyone was full
We all rested
Lying on the sofa
Soon it was bedtime
And Christmas was over.

Hayley Ker (14)
Kelso High School, Kelso

Bullying

An empty playground, everyone's with their friends.
One person walking alone, trying to meet his ends.
Hated by the rest, friendless.
The teacher won't comfort him. Why? Because he is the bully.

Jamie Norman (13)
Kelso High School, Kelso

Street Crime

Guns, racism, crime and fights why?
Why kill other people because of the colour of their skin?
Why shoot innocent people in the street because they're white
                                                    or black?

What sort of example is this to set?

America, supposedly the greatest country in the world,
Yet people from gangs drive around in their flash cars,
With their tinted windows
And chrome rims
And shoot innocent people.
Madness.

Where is George Bush?
Where is he when this is going on?
Starting wars!
Destroying America!
Totally unaware of what is going on!
Why?

Neil McGuigan (14)
Kelso High School, Kelso

Rainbow

The sun comes out
And the heavens open.
I wait for the rainbow to come.

I wait and wait,
And then here it comes,
Appearing through the clouds.
Red, orange, yellow, green, blue, indigo and violet.

I run and run to catch the rainbow,
But all I can see are clouds.
But then I see a gold shimmer and run for the pot of gold.

Lisa Jeffrey (12)
Kelso High School, Kelso

The War To End

A thud of the metal door -
The boat has reached the beach.
Oncoming bullets fly at us
As we crawl to the nearest trench
Not many of us make it that far.

I lay dripping, with the cold rain
Reminding me of where I am.
The captain comes to tell us a
New trench has been cleared.
I thrust my weakened legs
Up onto the sand.

Crawling, remembering to look for a clear shot,
I reach the trench.
A sharp stabbing pain in my leg,
I'm stunned; unable to move -
An arm reaches out for me -
It's my brother.

A medic pulls out a knife,
Digging into my leg, a bullet pops out
News is said that the captain is dead.
Anger in me takes over my pain.
I climb out of the trench onto the soggy sand.
Dodging flying bullets hiding behind a tank trap.

My leg starts to bleed; that doesn't stop me,
I reach the barbed wire
Cutting it open I charge in.
Behind me is a small group of troops following.
One is my brother.

I pull my sniper rifle out;
A sharp pain appears in my other leg
I fall down aiming;
I kill the gunner.
My brother is at my side
Something metal hits my side . . .

Scott Morris (13)
Kelso High School, Kelso

Guy Fawkes Night

On a cold November night,
The fifth is Bonfire Night,
Lots of people round the hot fire,
Laughing and fooling about,
The crackling of the fire,
Lots of people,
Little kids playing with sparklers,
The taste of the smoke in your mouth,
Queuing up for the free soup,
Too hot to drink,
The bangs of the fireworks,
Very loud,
Makes you jump,
And spill your soup.
Flashing bright fireworks in the night sky,
What a good display,
Cartwheels and different bangs,
Bright lights and different colours.

Michael Portsmouth (15)
Kelso High School, Kelso

Someone Special

I have his heart, he has mine,
Our love has no directions, no hint, no sign.
He looks at me with loving eyes,
Each time we touch brings butterflies.

Every kiss full of passion and sprinkled with love,
His beautiful smile from an angel above.
Never could anything tear us apart,
I'll hold him forever inside my heart.

No other could match or bring so much joy,
Every day that goes by makes us harder to destroy.
I know deep inside me my hero I've found,
My love for him is shown by feelings not sound.

Carmen Falla (13)
Kelso High School, Kelso

Battle

Bang!
The cannon is ready to go again
It has been lit
Bang!
Off it goes again,
It jolts back and forward.
Here comes a cannonball
Thud!
It hits the ground
In front of the row of cannons.
The sky is grey and dull
It is only afternoon
The battlefield is covered in dead bodies
All that can be heard is people shouting commands.
They have finished with the guns
In come the men with spears and swords
Both sides are now facing each other
Suddenly men with spears and swords are fighting
Screams of fear and pain come from both sides
Swords clanging together.
Thud! Thud! Thud!
More men falling to the ground
In come the horses galloping at full speed
Towards the mass of people
A huge black horse rears up
And falls to the ground
Hours have passed
Up comes a white flag
They have surrendered at last
It's the end of a long war
The battlefield is deserted
Full of dead people and horses
The smell of death is hanging
Around in the air.

Emma Thoms (13)
Kelso High School, Kelso

One Piece

His straw hat on his head, his crew ready to go
He sets sail for the grand line,
He is Luffy!
Luffy and his goofy laugh, strong spirit and hat
He ate the cursed gum gum fruit and now he is a rubber man
He can blow up like a balloon or stretch like a rubber band.

His sword's gleaming in the light,
His favourite green bandana on his head, he is ready to fight.
He is Zolo!
Zolo and his centauru, big ego and bad moods
He hates to lose to anyone, strikes as fast as an eagle in flight.

Her maps on her desk, her compass in her hand
She will navigate us through danger
She is Nami!
Nami and her expert navigating, thieving and secrets
She will navigate and negotiate us through thick and thin
With grace like a dove soaring.

His knees trembling, his sling-shot in hand
He will lead us into battle *not!*
He is Usopp!
Usopp and his long nose, sling-shot and fear
He hides in the shadows ready to pounce like a cat, or so he says.

His yellow hair blowing in the wind,
His lolly in his mouth,
His frying pan in his hand
He is ready to cook
He is Sanji!
Sanji and his cooking, flirting and curly eyebrows
He can cook up a storm
He will never waste food,
Never uses his hands to fight.

Yasmin Boni (14)
Kelso High School, Kelso

Aragorn

Picture him - dark brown hair, long brown cape
Symbolising the natural world
Whilst fighting the world of men.
A fellowship was forged to protect Frodo and the Ring
Tall and strong: Aragorn - the prominent protector.
He was born to be a king
Serious while in battle
Happy while feasting with friends.
His bravery is unmatched,
His courage is beyond measure,
His leadership skills are reliable as a true king,
Frodo was privileged to have him as a friend;
A trusting and loyal friend.

Robin Chapman (15)
Kelso High School, Kelso

War

Bang!
Shots fly around like headless chickens,
The sounds of the tank engines are in the background.
Boom!
Bombs drop on every living thing,
The midnight sky is an orange yellow colour,
Planes zoom overhead
Dropping bombs as they go,
People run as fast as they can,
To the bunkers they head
To seek shelter from the bombs
They sit tight
No one knows what will happen next.

Richard Marshall (13)
Kelso High School, Kelso

The Gamekeeper

Everything is quiet in the wet early morning,
Except for the gamekeeper in his big Land Rover
Whilst going along the quiet peaceful valley roads
Keeping an eye out
For the white-tipped tail menace
Known as the fox.
As he travels along the road
A white flash catches his eye,
He hears a rustling from the bushes
He takes his gun,
Loads it,
Cocks it,
Takes aim,
Bang!

Stuart Lowrie (14)
Kelso High School, Kelso

Autumn

As I looked out my window
I sensed the frozen feet feeling
And the cold nose sneezing,
I stepped out into the glistening sunlight
Onto the sparkling green mesh,
The crunching of the leaves beneath me was unreal,
It sounded like I was eating a bowl of cereal.
All I could feel was the soft, cosy cloth wrapped around my hands,
The quaking of my teeth in the cold morning air,
The gorgeous smell of clean air lurking,
The leaves twinkling in the yellow rays -
Golden red, orange and chestnut
Some as chestnut as a horse
I was the sort of day for soup -
I could feel it in the back of my clogged up throat.

Anna Ramsay (12)
Kelso High School, Kelso

Hallowe'en

Night-times
Dark and spooky
The only sound that can be heard
Is the wind
Whistling along the street,
Making the leaves rustle and
Crackle as they get blown along,
The trees swaying eerily,
Creating giant black shadows.

A new sound can be heard,
Kids laughing and squealing,
As they go trick or treating,
Kids getting frightened as they hear
Noises behind them.
Ghosts and witches everywhere,
Some with black cats following,
On behind.

Houses come into view,
Their gardens looking special,
Lanterns orange and bright,
Pumpkins turned into orange heads,
Hanging on tree branches,
Their flickering candles making
An eerie glow everywhere,
The night is set.

'Trick or treat!'

Jamie Heppell (15)
Kelso High School, Kelso

Outside The World

I sit on a seat.
I look out
The window,
I see my garden colours
Shooting out into my eyes;
Green, grey, pink.
Then,
I look up,
And see the mountains,
They are funny shapes -
Like teeth almost,
Grey and white,
Cold and fluffy.
But then I can't look up anymore -
I can't see.

There's nothing to see:
But nothing is something:

How can we tell that?
There isn't anything more -
Up, down, at the side,
Why do I want
To know?
Why do we show so much
Interest
In what's next?
I want to know;
We all do,-
But it's only
A matter of time.

Alexis Collins (12)
Kelso High School, Kelso

Bad Boy Rhyme

Nissan Skyline GTF
Wicked kit, a wicked car
Carbon fibre bucket seats
Wicked tunes and wicked beats
Bad boy bonnet, bad boy car
Come with me and you'll go far
Come with me and you will see
Dougy and the MCT
Look at me I am leading
One-hundred and ten is going speeding
On my car my tyre popped
Saw the police and then got stopped
In the jail I seen The T
MC-ing with the Dougy D
Got let out the morning after
That made me go even faster
Faster faster with the rhyme
Dougy D is doing his time
And this is how I end my rhyme
On this wicked ending line.

Paul Burke (14)
Kelso High School, Kelso

Music

The sound of an electric guitar,
Played loud and heavy,
The cymbals clanging as they
Are being hit by the edge of the drumstick,
The voice of the main singer,
Loud and angry and deep,
The bass guitar giving a rhythm beat
Throughout the song roaring and steady,
The playing of heavy metal is ear-splitting,
It gives me a feeling of forcefulness and freedom.

Thomas Gascoigne (15)
Kelso High School, Kelso

The Shooting

Bang! Bang!
The sky was as dark as a bottomless pit,
The street lights were dim.
The cobbles shone under the moon,
A man stood silently in the middle of the road
He barely moved.
He pulled out a gun -

Bang! Bang!
You could hear the laughter and joy coming out of the pub,
Three men walked out singing,
The silent man lifted his gun.

Bang! Bang!
A man fell helplessly,
His friends trying to help him,
The silent man stares,
The friends of the shot man cry.
The silent man places the gun to his head.
Bang! Bang!

Rachael Sudlow (14)
Kelso High School, Kelso

Hallowe'en

As night approaches
Darkness comes
People prepare for Hallowe'en
Carving their pumpkins
And buying their sweets
When night approaches
The kids come out
Ready for the night
Trick or treating
Throwing eggs
And causing havoc
All throughout the night.

Oliver Cunningham (15)
Kelso High School, Kelso

Autumn

As I stood in the grass
The autumn breeze hit me,
The golden leaves swept up
From the ground and flew past.
I walked forward,
Under my feet
I could feel the leaves crunching,
The howling, whistling wind
Blew past and took a tree from the roots.
It hit me. I fell.
I could taste the mouldy smell
Of the leaves,
I reached the park -
A bunch of boys were playing
With fresh conkers -
They had fallen from a chestnut tree,
I walked home through the forest,
The orange sap was oozing out of the trees,
I was tired after my autumn walk,
I had to go to sleep -
Goodnight.

Rebecca Corbett (12)
Kelso High School, Kelso

Bonfire Night

Bonfire Night is a sight to see
Just for you and me,
All the colours in the sky
Blue and purple for your eye,
All the rockets ever so high,
The smell of smoke fills the sky,
If you blink you miss the sight,
Bonfire Night is fading away!

Carol-Ann Noble (13)
Kelso High School, Kelso

Dance Of Danger

Whoosh!
A plane flying like a bird,
Dancing with another,
They spun and looped,
Looped and spun,
Firing the guns,
Trying to hit the other,
While trying to avoid being hit.

They climbed and dived,
Dived and climbed,
Trying to get the other,
Trying to stay alive,
One got a missile out -
Boom!
The other exploded!

No bail out!
He was dead!

The plane came back down to Earth the hard way -
It landed right on a building -
Crash!

The winner moved onto another plane,
The flames had engulfed the building and were spreading.

Boom!
A bomb went off -
The town was being destroyed;
Boom! Boom! Boom!

They were going to win,
It was raining bombs, making puddles of rubble.

Whoosh! Another plane came crashing down,
They started to retreat,
Leaving the destruction for today
To bring more tomorrow,
This was life in a war.

Dan Barnes (12)
Kelso High School, Kelso

Grass

These summer days after a days shopping on Princess Street,
When you just want to crash down onto the grass
It absorbing all your cares in the world.
The way you just can't lie still on it;
It's like lying on a mattress
A bed of wriggling hundreds and thousands.

The sight of it - sheer greenness
A green tarpaulin rolled over parks and hills
Stretched taut with the odd hole here and there
Where sharp rose gardens have pierced through
And heavy buildings have worn; like kneeling holes in a pair of jeans.

The smell of it - fresh and earthy with a zesty twist
When it's been freshly cut, its scent so purifying
Like breathing in a transparent beam of light.

Lightly licking the tips of grass blades is how a whisper would feel,
If you could touch one with your hands.
Grass whispering to us.
The tips of blades brushing the soles of your feet.
This feeling is like no other;
Rooted at the base of your mind's soul,
You'll never forget.

Emma Bain (15)
Kelso High School, Kelso

A Rainy Day

Rain is like a child crying,
Thunder is like desperate cries from lost souls,
Lightning bolts show how many will die that day,
Hailstones are like stones thrown from those who have died

before us,

A hurricane is the last chance for those who have done wrong in life,
An earthquake is the opening to Hell,
A rainy day can be the worst day of your life.

Laura Gibson (13)
Kelso High School, Kelso

The Knight

I ran out of the city gates with all the other men shouting behind me,
Arrows whistled by,
Taking down some of my men,
A siege weapon was fired,
Its roar was heard too late,
I fell to the ground,
I was pinned there,
The noise of men screaming in pain was awful.

The silence was deafening as everything seemed to stop at once,
I was dead to the world
For a moment
That felt like an eternity,
As I heard a ram on the city gates I got up,
As I ran I could hear the clashing of swords,
Spears impaling nearby men,
Horses galloping,
Men falling to their death.

My sword slashed across,
Killing the battering ram's crew,
I mounted my horse
And galloped towards the enemy general,
I rode him down with my cold iron sword,
I could taste his blood in the air,
My armour rubbed against my side
As I jumped off my horse.

The enemy morale was lowered,
I charged into them with my leather shield,
My sword gleamed,
Arrows rained down on us,
I smelt the blood and sweat,
Burning bodies lay all over the battlefield,
Thanks to our trebuchets,
Our archers had taken out everyone I didn't get to
Victory was ours.

John Scott (12)
Kelso High School, Kelso

Legend

The great Blue Wolf took for his wife the fair maiden Fallow Doe,
As she walked her life was taken by Dark Bear -
The young warrior saw her fall to the blackened arrow of the
                                                    Raven clan,
The warriors engaged and many men of both clans joined them,
Sounds of battle could be heard from afar.

The battle went on for three days straight
Until only the two tired young chiefs stood face to face,
Blue Wolf carried two axes now chipped and bloodstained,
Whilst the Bear carried two knives and a pale face's fire stick,
They fought long and hard
And found themselves at the waterfall -
The Great Bear, much stronger than the Blue Wolf,
Tossed him over the edge.

He grabbed the root hanging from the cliff beneath a ledge -
With great skill he tossed his axe, hitting the Bear in the back,
He plummeted and hit the ledge so hard it broke it,
It hit Blue Wolf and he fell, along with Dark Bear to Hell and back.

Matthew Fenwick (12)
Kelso High School, Kelso

The Eye Of The Storm

The rumble of the thunder,
The whistle of the wind,
The drumming of the wind like an army on parade,
The creaking of the trees bending in the wind,
The splashing and the screaming of people running home,
The winds are picking up now,
The wind is whipping at my coat,
My skin is beginning to sting as I get pelted by the rain,
I'd better run for cover.
The hurricane is coming.
I think I'll head home.

Andrew Dodds (13)
Kelso High School, Kelso

Fireworks

Lots of noise,
Big explosions,
These are some of the things you will hear,
The big *bang!*
Exploding in the sky,
With bright colours flashing in the darkness,
The rocket shooting up,
The moon,
With the stars in the blackness of the night,
Children with sparklers writing their name in the air,
All the colours you know,
Reaching high into the sky,
As the night gets late,
The fireworks start to get quieter and quieter.

Murray Hastie (13)
Kelso High School, Kelso

Being In Goal

Standing in the wooden goal the start whistle blows,
Lots of red and white Kelso strips running for the ball,
The ball is at the other end,
The goalie tries to kick it
But then
That sound of the heavy ball
Hitting the back of the wooden goal -
Victory!

We take centre again,
Straight away the ball is heading for me -
I go to kick it,
I hit it -
Everyone chases after it -
The end whistle blows.
We won!

Natasha Hewson (13)
Kelso High School, Kelso

Seasons

New life beginning,
Fresh green shoots
Springing from the ground.
Birds are singing
Cheerful songs
As baby lambs skip around their ewes.

Scorching hot sun
Smothering the ground,
The smoke from
Barbecue
Fills the air
As the long day
Fades into night.

Golden, crisp leaves
Tumble to the ground,
All shades of orange, gold
And red
Swirl in the air
As the cold wind
Nips your skin.

Faces shrouded
In misty breath,
Freezing fingers and toes,
Snowball fights
Run through the day,
And blizzards roar
At night.

Lucy Harding (12)
Kelso High School, Kelso

A Day At The Races

Nervous trainers, jockeys and owners,
Horses prancing around the collecting ring,
The spectators running to get their bets placed,
Trainers leading frantic horses onto the never-ending green track,
They all squeeze into their starting boxes fit to burst,
Everything goes silent then *bang!*
The gun has spoken,
The shouting and screaming began,
The commentator starts,
Bringing hope to some and despair for others,
Back on the track,
Jockeys whipping *snap! Snap! Snap!*
Nostrils flaring,
Foam spraying from their mouths,
Veins popping out beneath the skin,
'Two-hundred to go,' the commentator cries,
Only seconds to go,
The crowd goes wild,
They're neck and neck,
And Miss Matty Ross has got it.

The excitement's all over
The jockeys jump off and spray the champagne,
The steam rose off the horse's body,
Whilst the trainers throw their rugs on,
Miss Matty Ross in her loose box now
Twitching with excitement
Until the next time.

Jenny Brunton (12)
Kelso High School, Kelso

Manchester United

In Old Trafford the crowd sounds were high,
The stadium was packed full,
The game was set to start any minute.

The ref blew his whistle and the big Manchester derby had begun
Five minutes had gone,
No team had had a good attack yet.
Until Ruud van Nistelrooy was in the box,
He took the ball round the last defender and over the goalkeeper,
It just went past the post and out for a goal kick,
The goalie hoofed the ball up the park,
It came to Andy Cole,
He turned round and shot,
The ball curled round Edwin Van Der Sar and into the net,
Man City were winning!

At half-time it was two-one to Man United
Wayne Rooney had scored twice,
Man City brought the game to a draw
When Kieran Richardson put the ball into his own goal.

At the end of the game Man United had won four-two,
Wayne Rooney had scored his hat-trick and Ryan Giggs had scored.

Man United went top of The Premiership.

Stuart Skeldon (11)
Kelso High School, Kelso

The Battle

The battle begins -
It's the Romans against the Greeks.
The Roman Legions, red in all their glory
Attack the Greek Phalanxes.
The clash is strong enough to shatter shields.
Spears break, swords drawn, shields bash, arrows hit.

The horsemen and their generals charge to save their
surrounded men.

It's no use;
Their archers are in range
To continue on would certainly mean death.

But the battle rages on.

The kings pray to their gods to give them power and praise.

The Greeks retreat to an advantage point on a hill
But the Romans are smart,
And surround the hill
They begin to move upon the encircled Greeks.

The Greeks make a final stand
But can't withstand the Roman assault
They will not stand very long.

The Romans have won the bloody battle.

Scott Tonner (12)
Kelso High School, Kelso

The Trenches

(To all the men who died in this way)

The smell of the mud -
How awful it was,
The rotting of the bodies
Getting eaten by the rats,
Exploding bombs and shells
Filled the air with poisonous gas,
The sound of guns firing from our trenches.

Trenches; how dark and the mud was,
Cold was the water
That fell on our skin,
The sound of the guns,
Both big and small
Deafened my ears with that banging noise.

Then the smell of the gas
Filled my lungs
As I began to fall.

James Stewart (12)
Kelso High School, Kelso

Karate

Karate is not boring,
It's energetic and fun,
It's loud and will hurt in the morning,
But it's still a lot of fun.
You do a grading every three months,
You will hopefully pass every time,
It's sore on the legs and warm on the face,
You also do it at a very fast pace.
There are twenty belts,
All different colours,
Some have white stripes,
And one is pure white.

Jason Scott (11)
Kelso High School, Kelso

WWI The Western Front

The sight of my friends being shot,
Rotting in the mud of war.
Endless fighting -
Constant noise of *bang! Bang! Bang!*
And then *boom!* A shell exploding.
Then frantic gunfire
Machine gun fire
Mortars!
Shells!
And loads of dead bodies piled up.
Smoke hurtling into the air as supplies catch fire.

At night, dark, dingy, slippery,
Falling over dead bodies.
Noise at night is not so loud.

Planes during day
As they dash around in the sky -
One gets shot down,
The pilot falling to his death -
And then *bang!*
The plane hits the ground,
As it explodes, it is engulfed in flames.

Kevin Trotter (12)
Kelso High School, Kelso

Love

Love is the sun shining on a rainy day,
The pinkest of pink, the bluest of blue,
Chocolate sitting invitingly in a tin,
Your bed, warm in the morning,
A place of security at night,
The beating of your heart every time you see them,
The feeling when they hold you tight,
With all the angels coming closer,
Love is beauty, warmth and safety.

Louise Cowan (12)
Kelso High School, Kelso

Battle

I face the undefeated Vampaneze -
I look the purple-skinned scum in the eye,
I draw my sword from my sheath,
I raise it in the air and shout, 'Charge!'
Shouting insults come from behind me,
My men wave their weapons in the air,
We collide with the Vampaneze
I swing my sword at the closest enemy, killing it.

The Vampaneze are advancing on us,
My men are screaming, they are pleading,
My best friend is covered in Vampaneze blood,
Blood is flowing as swords clash together,
I'm still fighting, killing Vampaneze by the dozen.

The colour of blood red flowing everywhere,
I hear a familiar sound,
In terror I turn to see my best friend die in vain,
His killer is advancing on me -
I swing my sword heavily and bang
The Vampaneeze's head slides off its neck.

We are getting defeated -
My men are not retreating;
The Vampaneze are advancing on us -
I'm still fighting,
Swoosh! A big pain in my back arises -
A spear has gone through me,
My men are trying to help me, -
Our reinforcements arrive -
The Vampaneze runs.
I smile at myself and mutter, 'Victory!'

Then I die.

Kieran Flannigan (12)
Kelso High School, Kelso

Treesons

It's spring.
Start of a new year.
My buds turn to blossom.
My branches swarm with leaves.
Snowdrops grow all around me.
Lambs eat the grass beside me.
I love this time of year.
It's bright and jolly!

It's summer.
The sun beats down on me.
The birds sit on my branches for shade.
Bumblebees buzz around the flowers at my feet.
Families have picnics by the stream.
The blue snake winds through my friends and I.
I think this time of year is colourful and full of life.
I love it!

It's autumn.
My berries have started to ripen.
All of the leaves have turned yellow, red, orange and brown.
They cover the ground like a carpet of fire.
I get sad at this time of year.
I look ugly and dead.

It's winter.
I'm so cold.
Layers of white snow lie all around me.
There's no life in the valley now.
No lambs, no people, no nothing.
I have no leaves but my buds are starting to grow.
I'm so sad.
But I know that it's spring again soon.
I just think of that.

Stephanie Rae (12)
Kelso High School, Kelso

Bonfire Night

The bonfire was glowing -
The parents were laughing -
The kids were playing,
Fireworks were going off in my ear
Like a door slamming.

Everyone was watching the fireworks now,
Kids were playing with sparklers for fun,
The colours were bright;
They were really beautiful to watch.

The night was ending -
People were driving off in cars;
The fire was going out.

Back at home now,
My mum and me
Went to a fireworks display;
It was at the cobby.

I could smell burning,
I could see lights.
All my friends were there -
I was speaking to them.

It was all over -
I wish I could do it again.

Carly Green (11)
Kelso High School, Kelso

Leaves

The brilliant green leaves
Sparkle in the gleaming dew,
Firm and proud,
Clinging to the branch
In the cool spring wind.

Thick bushy branches
In the longer summer nights,
Cyclists flying by
Through the long shadows
Cast by the burning sun.

Brown and middle-aged,
Falling from the branches
To which they once so proudly clung,
Children stamping,
Kicking them up,
Once glorious, now cracked -
Once wonderful, now forgotten.

Bare-necked branches,
Covered white,
Hiding the scars
Of where the green used to stand
So long, long ago . . .

George Knox (13)
Kelso High School, Kelso

Autumn

Orange, red, brown;
Colours of the falling leaves,
Rustling as they break free
From the tree they used to belong to.

Leaves that have a crunchy noise when walked on,
A smell of dampness
That floats through the air.

Leaves are horrible;
The mess that they leave behind
A poor soul has to clean up.

Leaves are nice to look at,
With lovely colours.
They can be dangerous
When wet,
Fun to play with
When dry.

Gillian Forsyth (12)
Kelso High School, Kelso

It's That Time Of Year

It's Christmas time again.
It's that time of year.
When the leaves fall off the trees
And the snow starts to fall.
Yes, it's that time of year.
The time of year everyone loves.
With the giving and taking.
It's fun, it's nice, it's a happy time of year.
Building the snowmen,
Sculpting the snowmen.
It's a happy time of year.
When Santa comes and does his stuff,
It's a really good time of year!

Fraser McFarlane (12)
Kelso High School, Kelso

Snow

Everything is white,
At night it is quite bright -
Colourful sledges coming down the hills,
Cardboard boxes lying everywhere.

Boots and the snow crunching together,
Screaming children playing snowball fights.

Air is fresh -
Fresh cold smell.

People wearing coloured Wellingtons,
Nice warm matching hats, scarves and gloves.
Looks like they are very cosy with their woolly jumpers on.

Very cold ground,
Smooth bits
Bumpy bits -
Lumps of snow everywhere.

I see people crashing into snow,
People flying over snow bumps,
Snowballs over there,
And snowballs in the air.

Michelle Ewart (12)
Kelso High School, Kelso

School

The school playground is filled with rubbish
Bins are dirty and wet
The corridors are filled with kids running
Teachers are angry with stress
The canteen smell
Makes you feel so hungry
The people are so warm and friendly
The school and flowers outside
Blossom with glory
For I am the headmaster and proud.

Laura Thomson (13)
Kelso High School, Kelso

Christmas

It's a cold frosty morning
I lie in my bed stiff as an ice cube
I look outside my window and I see snow
I turn on the TV everyone is shouting merry christmas1
I think I'm only dreaming.

Suddenly I'm full of life
I jump up and run down the stairs
My mum, dad and sister are waiting for me to open my presents.

Then I hear bells
Bing, ding, ding and *ding!*
'Is it Santa?' I shout
I run outside, I see Santa
Where's the reindeer I ask
I go inside with devastation
But I'm not upset
I still have presents to open.

I go inside
I smell the fresh cooked turkey
I can see the lights that twinkle in my eye
I open all my presents
I thank my family for them.

I really loved my Christmas
I hope you like yours too
Remember to say thanks for your presents
Especially Santa Claus and all the reindeer for bringing them to you,.

Debbie Todd (13)
Kelso High School, Kelso

Hallowe'en

'Argh!'
The little boy heard it,
A scream,
Are there real ghosts?
It's Hallowe'en after all.

Everywhere is dark and gloomy
Monsters,
Ghouls,
Ghosts,
Even the evil Grim Reaper,
Everybody can see and hear them,
People running everywhere,
Trying to get away.

An icy hand,
It's holding onto the little boy's shoulder,
And then he hears it,
'Ho, ho ha ha ha,'
The boy shivers and starts to run.

He hears music behind him -
'Do da do do, do da do do'
He turns round and sees -
There's the Ghost Busters!
They charge their weapons and
Suck up all the ghosts
It is now a normal Hallowe'en
The smell of candy is back.

Josh Hogarth (11)
Kelso High School, Kelso

Rainbow

Rainbow, rainbow
I see you in the sky
Your colours are bright
They shine all the time
Your colours mean so much
The reds, yellows, oranges -
They mean sun
Blues, purples, greens -
They mean rain
The way the light shines
I like it very much
You can't hear it
You can't touch it
All you can do is see it
When I see one
I always like it
It's funny
The rainbows only ever come out when
One minute the sun is shining
And the next minute
It is raining
That is how a rainbow is made.

Emma Jeffrey (12)
Kelso High School, Kelso

Run

He ran and ran
Only to find his soldiers
Giving their lives
Away
For his friends and family.

He ran and ran
Only to find his soldiers
Dead.

He ran and ran
Only to find his planes
Have been shot
Down.

He ran and ran
Only to see
His friends once
Again.

Michael Purves (13)
Kelso High School, Kelso

Fireworks

Bang!
There goes a rocket,
A bright flash of yellow,
The smoke in the air.
Your eyes blinded by the bright colours,
The taste of smoke in your mouth,
Catherine wheels spinning,
Sparklers sparking blues and reds,
The bright colours of fountains blind your eyes,
Other loud bangs in the distance,
As it gets late the bangs get quieter.

Kevin Dryden (12)
Kelso High School, Kelso

A Teardrop

It is difficult to just let go,
Not to pretend or fake a smile
Just let your feelings take control -
It feels really good to cry.

When no one is on your side
A sad film
Someone's died -
It feels really good to cry.

To hold a teddy bear really tight,
You want attention,
You've had a fight -
It feels really good to cry.

I listen to a sad song,
I want,
I need,
I long, I long,
I really need to cry.

Celia Ledgerwood-Walker (13)
Kelso High School, Kelso

Snow

It's so exciting when snow falls,
Especially on Christmas Day,
There is so much fun to have,
Sledging snow fights and snowmen.

Snow is white and cold,
It is soft but ice can be hard,
You can ski or snowboard,
And make snow angels.

But then the sun comes out,
And melts the snow,
So we'll have to wait,
Until it snows next year.

Jordan Reid (13)
Kelso High School, Kelso

Football

The goal nets ripple in the wind
The players come out of the tunnel
The fans go wild
The flashy boots step onto the pitch
The whistle goes
The clock starts
The red card comes out
The stadium goes quiet
The ball crashes off the bar
The fans get nervous
The super sub comes on
He gets right into the action with a crunching tackle
The ball breaks for him
He hits a venomous shot
That cruises into the top corner
The whistle goes; the fans give a sigh of relief.

Ewan Whittle (13)
Kelso High School, Kelso

Snow

White and pure,
It lies on the ground like a thick blanket
Children jump excitedly,
Grabbing their sleighs
And running towards the hill
Raging snowball fights take place
The icy wind blows loose flakes into your eyes
It crunches like gravel underneath the footsteps
Of the playing children
Is it from the clouds or the heavens?
Is it frozen water or magic dust?

But it must end
The grey sky will clear; turning to blue,
The once tall, proud snowman will melt
Leaving only water in its place.

Peter Watson (13)
Kelso High School, Kelso

Fairytale

Candyfloss clouds and large magnificent castles
Herds of unicorns graze in the crystal fields
Fairies flutter in the forest singing sweetly for all to hear
Princesses skip through meadows collecting bunches of flowers
While handsome Prince Charmings seek to find their true love.

In Far, Far Away live all the famous celebrities;
At house number three lives Little Red Riding Hood and
                                                  Grandma Wolf
At house number four lives Hansel and Gretel
Rapunzel sits on a toadstool combing her golden-brown locks
As Dorothy and Toto follow the yellow brick road.

Rainbows dazzle in the blue skies,
Sparks of magic glisten up high
Dwarves and gnomes build little wooden tree houses
And mermaids bathe on a rock near the waterfall
Joy, pleasure and warmth fill the air.

The Fairy Godmother is the Queen of Fairytale
Caring and loving like any other queen would be,
King Charming, her beloved husband,
Brave and protective, and respected by his people
It's a friendly little country where I'd love to be.

No one knows actually where Fairytale is -
But what we do know is, it's a place full of magic and fantasy,
Some people say it's hidden at the bottom of the sea,
Others say it's your imagination that takes you there, -
I believe in Fairytale: do you?

Amy Nichol (12)
Kelso High School, Kelso

Derby Game

The fireworks go off,
The flares are lit.
The captains shake hands and make their peace,
But then it is broken by a furious battle.
The ball skims around like skates on ice,
Tackles slide in from everywhere.
High balls are played into the box
From the cheetahs on the wing.
New flashy boots gleam on the floodlit pitch.
The woodwork is hit by a powerful shot and all the action happens
in the box.

Fans cheer for their team,
The coaches' frantically shout and yell,
Instructions coming from every fan.
The referee gets loads of stick
As he sends a player off for a scrap in the box.
A penalty is given to the whites,
The hero steps up to take the shot.
He feels sick inside,
He feels he will miss,
But he slots it away in the bottom corner.
The fans go wild and jump around,
The stadium is full of sound.
Only a few minutes left -
A last minute scramble in the box
Leads to a last minute penalty.
The striker steps up and puts it over.
This has ended the game
And his reputation.

Thomas Rothwell (13)
Kelso High School, Kelso

Fireworks

Bang!
Colour bursting out,
Blues, reds, yellows
All the colours in the sky,
Whistling up into the sky
Bang!
Spark!
The fireworks crackle
People chucking sticks in the fire,
Snap! Crackle! Pop!
Fire blazing!
All shapes and sizes of logs burning away
You smell the gunpowder of the fireworks
Bang!
You can smell the food
That people have made and are eating,
You taste
The smoke of the fireworks
In your mouth.

David Richardson (13)
Kelso High School, Kelso

World Cup Glory

As you take your first step to World Cup glory
The crowd have turned up in their thousands to watch.
Your adrenalin is pumping as a lightning flash.
The atmosphere is electric and buzzing like an angry bee.
You can hear the crowd chanting and cheering every second
of the game.
Singing as you're winning it keeps you going.
The feeling of winning is now indescribable.
The joy, the pleasure, it stays forever.
It's the time of your life.

Ross Henderson (13)
Kelso High School, Kelso

The Last Soldier

The city is devastated,
By explosions,
And gunfire.
The city is dark and dingy.
Fear; the city is rank with it.

A single soldier hides behind,
He wants to be home,
To see his family.

But he cannot remember their faces,
Nor the smell of flowers,
Or the touch of grass,
Only rough, cold stone,
And suffering.

With a bitter taste in his mouth,
He stands up, turns round
To see the enemy front.
Lifeless soldiers,
And monstrous tanks.

He charges towards the enemy,
To his doom,
Or to theirs.

Chris Laidler (13)
Kelso High School, Kelso

Friends

When you're upset and when you are down
Your friends are there to show you they care
They might speak to you one day and not the next
But at the end of the day they will always come back
Friends don't care if you're fat, thin, small or tall
But if they do they're not your friends at all
If you get a good friend never let them go
Keep in touch wherever they go.

Katie Craig (13)
Kelso High School, Kelso

War

Ching!
A bullet bounces off my helmet;
I can feel a dent,
Boy am I lucky,
It didn't hit me in the head!

I run along the beach front
Grabbing ammo as I go,
I dive into a trench,
As I watch my friends explode!

Bang!
An allied plane drops a bomb
That kills so many people,
A soldier dives in next to me,
He asks me what to do!

I tell him not to worry,
Just to keep his head down,
If he sticks with me,
He'll be OK!

We both start running,
Towards the frontline.
I make it -
But the allied soldier lost his life.

We dig holes,
Stick blow tubes in them -
Bang! The tubes explode,
We're past the fence.

I break into the building.
Kill a man in cold blood!
'Halt! Who goes there?'
I don't reply.
An enemy soldier,
I'm about to die!

Matthew Bell (13)
Kelso High School, Kelso

Christmas

You wake up early in the morning
You go and wake everyone else in the house
You run down the stairs
Go into the living room
Find your pressies
You open the biggest one first
You open the rest
Take them to your room
Your bedroom is a mess
You go and get dressed
Go to get in the car
It is freezing
You go in the car to Gran's to get tea
You walk in
You smell everything cooking
It smells nice
You give her a present
Your cousins come
You give them their presents
They give you yours.

Deeanne Gay (13)
Kelso High School, Kelso

To A Doggy

My wee mutt canny as anything.
Yee stare at me, way gin ee
I can tell you can still taste yer meat.
Yip! Yip! Yee! Bank as t smell
Your shampoo little mutt
Black and white
Yee feel as soft and silky
You're huggable as can be noo
Where wid a be without ma wee dug?

Aron Graham (12)
Kelso High School, Kelso

Queen Regina

(I play this character in 'The Changeling Princess')

I am Queen Regina
I am very proud and loyal
My children are wonderful,
Except one, the changeling
We all call her
Very stupid.

I have lots of courtiers
Who chose my clothes,
Polish my shoes.
My husband King Edmond
Is a bit dopey
He runs around the palace
Trying to fix his kingdom.

I am very royal,
I have a shimmering tiara.
And a big shiny diamond necklace.

My throne is very big
And beautiful,
If I do say so myself.
My cook, Mrs Bundle
Is always chasing
This boy Fred
For stealing her
Jam tarts.

I am the queen;
Every room I go into
People bow down to me.

Victoria Lowrie (13)
Kelso High School, Kelso

Rainbow Jumper

I love my rainbow jumper
It has seven colours clear.
A colour for every day of the week
And every week of the year.

Red is bold, for danger and passion,
A blood-red sunset filling the sky.
Orange is fruit, on orange trees growing
Deep in the jungle where tigers lie.

Yellow is happy, the colour of sunshine,
Wearing yellow will bring you a smile.
Green is leafy, the colour of nature
Endless forests stretching for miles.

Blue is calm, a clear sky above us
Mighty waves crashing, the swell of the sea.
Indigo exotic, deep, full of meaning
The colour of spirits and mystery.

Violet is hazy, the colour of flowers
Pansies, foxgloves and lavender too.
Together these colours will make up a rainbow
Red through to violet on a canvas of blue.

I love my rainbow jumper
It has seven colours clear.
A colour for every day of the week
And every week of the year.

Faye Harland (15)
Kelso High School, Kelso

Snow

The frost is lacing its way up my arms,
Its icy fingers chilling me to the bone,
I feel like the only person left in the world,
Surrounded by a sea of white.

All I can see in the mass of white are my footprints,
Stretching as far as the eye can see;
Little dimples in the shimmering snow.

Icicles hanging everywhere
Trees standing old and crippled.
Thick with snow,
Clouds looming menacingly overhead.

My feet are tingling with the cold;
It's getting dark,
I look up and see swirling snow floating down towards me,
It's hypnotising,
I stand still just watching . . . waiting.

Freya Fullarton (13)
Kelso High School, Kelso

Fall

Fall has finally arrived,
A year ago it was the same time.
All the leaves have fallen off the trees,
Lying in a heap of bright colours.

The wind and rain have finally come,
With the rain battering off the windows.
The wind is like little kids,
Pulling off the leaves of the trees,
And kicking them about.

Fall is the time for romance,
With the beautiful trees and the romantic sunset
Oh what a great time of year!

Eilidh Mitchell (13)
Kelso High School, Kelso

Winter

I love winter
I love winter because
It is a time
For Christmas and presents
And lots and lots of snow!
The best thing about Christmas is
Throwing snowballs at other people
Another best thing is decorating the Christmas tree!
Winter is like a freezer
Cold, dark, cloudy!
The sun doesn't appear from behind the clouds.
The sun is lost and lonely.
The trees are bare
Lost and lonely and don't
Know where to go.
Winter is a wonderful season to have,
Winter is a time for families
To get together.

Adele Nicol (13)
Kelso High School, Kelso

The Black Templars' Crusade

Fighting for the Emperor,
In the name of Dorn.

Close-combat terminators
Hold their weapons in a terrifying stance.

Land raider Crusader,
Destroys everything in its path.

The scout squad spots an advancing army of chaos space marines,
A direct hit destroys the defiler.

The Black Templars have purified another planet,
But how long will the peace last?

Danny Bennet (13)
Kelso High School, Kelso

The Garden!

I can see the flowerbed of colour,
The buzzy bee collecting pollen,
The smell of the flowers making the air smell great.

I can hear the trampoline springs screeching,
The children laughing and giggling,
The smiles on their faces are magical.

I can smell the fresh cut grass,
The neighbour's lawnmower buzzing,
The birds flying with fright.

I can feel the cool breeze brushing my face,
The blue cloudless sky,
The sound of the birds tweeting tickles my ears.

I can see the guinea pigs running about in the cage,
The guinea pigs are squeaking and purring,
I can hear them munching.

Claire Henderson (12)
Kelso High School, Kelso

Autumn

Golden layers cover the ground
Squelching under my boots
As I walk Saisha through the drizzling mist
A strong breeze flowing towards me

I can smell the fresh crispness of the air,
The cold wind upon my face
The crunch of leaves beneath my feet
Leaves rustling in the trees

I can hear the rain patting on the ground
And splashing in the puddles around me
The leaves float by on the river
As I finish my walk through the mist.

Robert Griffin (17)
Kelso High School, Kelso

Helm's Deep

The cannon booms in the valley of Helm's Deep,
Before the soldiers moaning and screaming from the pain
Can be heard above the battle cries,
The stench of the death hangs in the air
Just above the smoke that fills my lungs
I tremble with fear as I prepare for battle;
My cold sweaty hands grasp the smooth metal sword
As the cold rain hits hard on my face.
I look out over the battle I must join.
The bright lights of the golden fires shine in my eyes
I see row upon row of soldiers in grey armour
Surging forward
I look around - there's no one here to help me
As many crumple to the muddy ground - screaming.
The black night gives no light.
Until, I look to the hills and see a shining light,
Gandalf the White had come to save us!
My nerves disappear and I rush to the battle
And victory over the evil Orcs!

Louise Chapman (13)
Kelso High School, Kelso

Mayhem School

The clock is ticking, tick-tock, tick-tock
It's only three more minutes until the end of the day
Suddenly I hear the bell go and mayhem lets loose
In the corridor everyone is pushing their way down the stairs and

out the door

But suddenly someone falls down the bottom steps
Everyone is laughing at her
But it's okay, she's laughing too
Finally out in the open air and almost home
I am finally home now and everything is quiet
I now settle down and do my homework
I get my things ready for another day at mayhem school!

Zoe Waddell (11)
Kelso High School, Kelso

The Stalker

Leaves are crunching behind me;
I turn my torch on -
There he is
It's the masked man!

It's the man from my dreams -
He starts to chase me;
I run, but he catches me
He's got a knife.

He puts the cold, sharp knife against my throat.
I freeze.
Am I going to die?
He whispers in my ear.

'You're going to die.'
I have to do something
I flip him over my back,
He just lies there like a statue.

I pick up the knife,
Should I slit his throat?
I put the knife against his throat,
But no, I'll not be a murderer.

I pick up the phone and call the police
I leave the knife on the ground,
I turn my back to him, he wakes up,
He picks up the knife and . . .

Paul Blacklock (13)
Kelso High School, Kelso

Seasons

Spring is cool, crisp mornings,
Newborn lambs bouncing over the fields,
It's trees growing
Leaves and flowers appearing
From beneath the ground.

Summer is the sun
Sitting high up in the sky,
Roasting you alive,
As you lie on the beach,
It's people who are happy,
And a smile on their face.

Autumn is pouring rain
And gale-force winds,
Blowing leaves off the trees
It's kicking the leaves
Up in the air
And letting them shower over you
As they flutter back down.

Winter is snowflakes and ice
Shimmering in the winter sun,
It's going sledging
With your friends
And sitting by the fire
On cold, dark nights.

Claire Blacklock (16)
Kelso High School, Kelso

The Best Friends In The World

Friends are the best!
They can multitask:
Be a shoulder to cry on
'Sob! Sob!'
And can make me laugh
'Ha! Ha!'

We can share secrets
'Sssh don't tell!'
Their style is amazing
And they are too.

They are walking problem pages,
But are loads of fun too.
Although we like different things,
They are my friends now
And they will be forever
Forever!

Lauren Dickson (13)
Kelso High School, Kelso

Summer

Summer is here
The holidays have begun
Topping up the tan
As the heat has begun.

Out with our friends
As the laughter begins
Laughing and joking
Till the night comes to an end.

The holidays are ending
And the summer has come to an end
So let's say goodbye
To all our good friends.

Rebecca Crawford (14)
Kelso High School, Kelso

Boredom

Sitting here
Nothing to do
I'm bored, I'm bored!

Look out the window
Grey, dull rain
It's falling, it's falling!

Eyes closing
Head dropping
I'm yawning, I'm yawning!

Time standing still
And so am I, but
It's ticking, it's ticking!

Sitting here
Nothing to do
I'm bored, I'm bored!

Faria Bhuiyan (14)
Kelso High School, Kelso

The Dream Of A Lifetime

Trees swaying in the wind,
Squeaking as they move.
My horse Misty Fever,
Cantering in the forest not even scared
But me I was scared, I was terrified.
It was getting dark
I did not know where I was,
Where I was heading.
I reached the end
There was fresh water, beautiful stones.
It was great, I was not scared
There was a stable and a shed with a bed.
It was like it was a miracle.
But it was one great big *dream.*

Suzanne Gray (12)
Kelso High School, Kelso

My Outfit

A pink top with sequins.
Blue and pink checked skirt.
Sits on my chair waiting.
It's for a party.
I've been waiting patiently to put my outfit on all day.
I hope everyone likes it.
The party's at school.
My friends aren't going but I am.
I walk into the hall.
I can see the bright lights.
I smile.
I'm here.
But nobody else is.
I see a poster on the notice board.
Come to the coolest party of the year.
Invites only.
I understand where my friends are.
We stand.
My outfit and me.
The only real friend I have.

Kerry Dickson (13)
Kelso High School, Kelso

Friends

Friends forever we will be
No matter what gets in our way
What can I do to make you see
That friends are more important than boys?
Friends are for life, boyfriends come and go
Friends are special
So don't let them go
You will always need them
Friends forever we will be.

Alison Dumma (14)
Kelso High School, Kelso

I Don't Like Hospitals

I lay there in the sun,
Watching everybody having fun.
I lay there in the sun,
Nobody is looking glum.

I lay there in the rain,
Watching everybody going through pain.
I lay there in the rain
Nobody is going through the strain.

I lay there at night
Watching everybody looking with fright.
I lay there at night
Everybody looking to their left, then looking to their right.

I don't like hospitals.

Natasha Pattinson (14)
Kelso High School, Kelso

Anger

When you're angry you don't think before you speak
Your body tenses up
Your hands make fists
You shout and don't care what people think
You take deep breaths but you can't concentrate
You're too angry to think
You try to calm down but you can't
Anger is a hard thing to control
That's what I think anger feels like
If anger really gets to you, you hurt yourself but you really don't care
You have to get it out of you
You go mad and shout and shake
Until you get it out
Everyone is an enemy, your family and friends.

Hayley Bennet (14)
Kelso High School, Kelso

Winter's Here

It's a cold winter's night,
I hear a tip-tap sound at the window,
A ghost, a women, a man, what is it?
I can smell burning,
It looks like a plant,
Or maybe even an animal,
But I can't be sure,
I get closer to explore,
I flinch as I open the blinds,
As I back away,
It disappears,
I can't hear anything,
I begin to reassure myself that it was nothing,
When suddenly
My mum and dad walk in,
What's going on?
I sit shaking,
Speechless.

Shelley McBlain (12)
Kelso High School, Kelso

Autumn Leaves

Leaves, leaves all around
Leaves, leaves on the ground
Spread across the pavements
Scattered along the street
These leaves are not so very neat
Then it comes to spring
Again the leaves upon
The trees blowing in
The wind. Shivering in
The breeze.

Laura Noon (14)
Kelso High School, Kelso

Fireworks

One cold, frosty night,
I heard this big bang,
The light shone through the window,
The big bang exploded,
I thought fireworks, *wow!*

I go outside,
I see the bright colours,
The colours I see are red, orange and yellow.

The fireworks are fab,
The rockets and Catherine wheels are going off,
There are lots more fireworks,
Rockets are the best.

The fireworks stop,
I go inside,
Look out of the window,
It must be the end of the night,
I go back to bed.

Kerry McVie (12)
Kelso High School, Kelso

I Got Rhythm!

So much noise
So much fun
So much freedom
On the drums

Cymbal to the right
Hi-hat to the left
Without the rhythm
I am bereft

Sticks for the toms
Make sure the snare is on
Pedal for the big bass
Rhythm is my case.

Allie Young (14)
Kelso High School, Kelso

Fireworks

At night,
All the fireworks getting set up,
They get lit,
They shoot up
Around the sky,
All the bright colours exploding with colours,
Bursting and then exploding again
Into a series of colours - reds, yellows, blues and green
The sounds popping and banging
The Catherine wheels spinning
With yellow sparks flying out of the side,
The noise of the hissing sparks
Men shouting, 'Keep clear' because they are
Lighting up some exploding fireworks -
Great big explosions
The colours going from
White to yellow
With a red tinge to it.

Andrew Thomson (12)
Kelso High School, Kelso

What's That Noise?

There's a knock at the door
The door creaks open
The wind howls in
As I stand there's two witches
'Trick or treat! Trick or treat!
Give me something good to eat.'
Their faces are covered in make-up
As they stand the pumpkin flickers
As the girl holds it
They hand out their buckets
I look in their buckets,
There was sweets and money
The sweets clattered in the box
As I put it in
The girls say thanks
As they walk away
There was a clip-clop
I slammed the door
What was it?

Terri Wight (12)
Kelso High School, Kelso

Call Of Duty

The dust settles,
Floating to the ground like snow.
Flames lick the walls of the house.
All are dead -

Raining fire onto roofs,
Only defence a flimsy umbrella.
Somewhere else people sleep tight,
Not in this town.

Tides of men crash against defences,
In a desperate flair to win the battle.
Their blood spills and is washed aside,
Behind these dead; more soldiers stand.

Bullets rip and shrapnel flies,
Shattering bones,
Scurrying like rats
The men hide in trenches.

Ian Henderson (16)
Kelso High School, Kelso

Anger

Arghhhh!

I clench my fists as hard as a rock
My face automatically screws itself up
A smell of burnt biscuits fills the air
And a smell that could only be described as barbecued hair
I feel like a huge firework about to explode
My mouth tastes like undiluted coffee powder
Bitter
A bit like my thoughts
All I see is black with silhouettes of people
My matted hair is standing on its feet
Suddenly all my anger floods out of me

My sister's handed me back my pencil.

Fiona Black (12)
Kelso High School, Kelso

White Vs Black

The cackle of her laugh
The tormenting phrases she uses
The fear in my eyes
Too scared to move
Why should I get hurt just because I'm black?

I run home, but always get tripped up
I get pulled to the ground by my hair
I get kicked in places that my clothes cover
Threatened if I say a word, things will get worst
Black and blue I sit at home crying
Why should I get hurt just because I'm black?

Scared to go out of the house
I don't
Why me?
It's just too much to handle anymore
I'm just a coward
I shouldn't be scared to go out
But I am
Why should I get hurt just because I'm black?

I sit silently in my room until I fall asleep, awaiting another day
Tears streaming down my face, hitting the pool on the floor
Am I going to live like this forever?
I can't just stay here - like this forever!
I'll hide
Why should I get hurt just because I'm black?

Another day arises - I don't want to get up
How will I ever survive another day?
I won't!
I will stand up and speak out!
Why should I get hurt just because I'm black?

Why did my daughter have to get hurt just because she's white?

Ashley Gibson (16)
Kelso High School, Kelso

Beat Bullying

Day in, day out
The bully lurks about.
The terror in his eyes
The laughter from his mouth
I run off and cry.

Chased down the lane
Unsure of what lay ahead.

I attempted to make a run, through deep nettles
But ended up being stung.
Running through the pain
I ended up falling to the ground.
The bully stood above me.

Bang! Out for the count
Blood all around me,
Staining through my clothes onto my skin.
I pulled myself together
But that wasn't enough.

My life had been ruined,
Scarred for life
I would never forget that day.

Craig Edwards (16)
Kelso High School, Kelso

I Love You

I love you
I love you because of who you are
I love you because of who I am when I'm with you
I love you because of what we are
I love you.

I love you
I love the way you smile
I love the way you hold my hand like you'll never let go
I love the way you laugh
I love you.

I love you
I love your eyes
I love the feeling of your warm breath on my face
I love your kiss
I love you.

Most of all I need you . . .

I need you
I need you to cuddle me
I need you to wipe the lonely tears from my eyes
I need to you love me
I need you.

Becki Callander (15)
Kelso High School, Kelso

Fireworks

Everything is dark -
Everyone is talking,
Waiting for it to appear:
They start to look at the sky.

There is a sudden *bang!*
A flash of light -
The colours dazzle the sky,
People fall silent,
Just gazing at the sky.

The colours fade away -
People start talking again,
The children are playing games.

The sky has gone back to being dark,
Everyone is talking,
Waiting for it to appear:
They start looking at the sky.

Helena Dellow (17)
Kelso High School, Kelso

Rain

Small specks of water
Start to fall from the
Sky all shooting down
As if the clouds begin
To cry

Umbrellas start to open
People begin to run
Sheltering from the wet
Hoping for some sun

Eventually it stops
And a rainbow appears
Gradually getting brighter
As the dull day clears

Everybody's happy
Even the birds start to sing
Puddles begin to shimmer
Like the crown of a king.

Verity Falconer (14)
Kelso High School, Kelso

Hockey

The early mornings
The long but fun bus journeys
On the pitch
The butterflies in my stomach before the game starts
The numbness of hands
The harsh winter air blowing in your face
The refs whistle announcing the start of the game
The sour oranges at half-time
The swapping of sides
The thrill of winning
Or more often the pain of defeat
The three cheers for whoever
The shaking of hands
Maybe a bruised leg or arm
But it was all worth it
Now it's all over till next week.

Rebecca Stewart (14)
Kelso High School, Kelso

Wind

The wind does breathe
The wind does live
The wind is something in the air

The whistling wind in my ear
Breathing down the cold long
Days

What colour is the wind?
What colour?
What colour?

Colourless, but textured
Tickling, teasing and ruffling
Your hair, clothes
And skimming skin
That's nipped and beaten.

Emma Graham (14)
Kelso High School, Kelso

Autumn

There's an autumnal feeling in the air
A cool chill catching you unaware after the warmth of summer.
A brisk breeze sends bronze, red and yellow leaves
Swirling and fluttering around.
Then they fall back to the ground,
Motionless, until another gust of wind
Sets them off into another merry dance.
A season stuck between two extremes of weather,
The sun, heat and glow of summer
And the cold, dark, frosty days of winter
Are linked together by autumn.
Summer is behind us and days are becoming shorter,
Winter is coming.
The smoke of burning leaves can be smelled in the air,
Tall plumes of smoke reach high into the sky,
Only to be caught by the cool wind and is dispersed into nothing.
There's an autumnal feeling in the air
One that comes around each year.

Sophie Robeson (15)
Kelso High School, Kelso

The Forest

Surrounded by fields of crops stands the forest
Mighty trees poking out into the sky.
Branches reaching out like arms linking onto one another.
Tiny drops of dew sit like pearls on the leaves.
The trees dance as the wind brushes past.
Younger trees begin their struggle to reach the light.
Rising slowly from the ground their journey begins.

Victoria Grant (14)
Kelso High School, Kelso

Nothing

Nothing is nothing
Nothing is boring
Nothing is sometimes okay
Nothing can be sleeping
Nothing can be tiring
Nothing can be endless
Nothing can be only 2 minutes
Nothing can make you sleep
Nothing can drive you up the wall
Nothing can drive you to insanity
Nothing can make you angry
Nothing can be horrible
Nothing could take over your life
Nothing is like being at school
Nothing could make you do something
Nothing makes me do something
To stop me being bored and
Stop doing nothing.

Ross Gillie (14)
Kelso High School, Kelso

Weather

Pitter-patter, pitter-patter goes the rain
Wet, cold and clear
Tap, tap, tap go the hailstones
Hard to the touch
Nothing - you can't hear a sound as the snow floats around
Soft and gentle, but cold to the touch
Beaming down cheerfully is the sun
Happy, bright and warm
Strong and fierce is the wind
Blowing round all the leaves.

Heather Portsmouth (12)
Kelso High School, Kelso

Just Friends

You say you want to be just friends
But do you mean goodbye?
Is that the easy way to end
The wish without the why?

You owe me nothing, as I owe
You equally, and yet
There's something in the undertow
I cannot just forget

There's something lovely like a song
That's waiting to be heard
Or like the feelings that belong
To some unspoken word

And so with you I cannot simply
Smile and stay sweet
I take the risk of asking frankly,
For the untold truth.

Amy Wilson (15)
Kelso High School, Kelso

Fireworks

Fireworks
The blazing maze of
Patterns of colours
Smells of gunpowder
Bursts of explosions
Whistling of the rockets
Colourful rings and sounds
Pops, bangs, snaps and crackles
Fountains and fountains of colour
Reds, blues, green, oranges, purples
The fuzzy patterns as they fade away.

John Grant (12)
Kelso High School, Kelso

Make A Wish

Make a wish and you will see
You can be whoever you want to be
A fairy princess or an African queen
A giant banana or a runner bean
A superhero or theme park owner
A teddy bear or the world's biggest moaner
A famous superstar or jewellery designer
A Christmas elf or a gold miner
A millionaire or flower fairy
The world's youngest rock star or a witch who is scary
A snake in the desert or a bird flying high
An Olympic gymnast or a star in the sky
A pure white horse or a demanding diva
A cat or a girl with shopping fever
Make a wish and you will see
Your child inside needs to be free.

Fiona Hunter (15)
Kelso High School, Kelso

Hallowe'en

Hallowe'en is fun:

Throwing eggs and water balloons
Getting sweets and money
People shouting and screaming
Listening to jokes
Everyone running and running

Getting hit by eggs and water balloons
Orange glow coming from lanterns
People dressed up as witches
See blood pouring from people's mouths
Horrible smell of stink bombs -
Rotten eggs smell the town out

Hallowe'en is fun.

Daniel Bennet (12)
Kelso High School, Kelso

Work - Not For The Faint Hearted!

Early morning when I get up
I look like death warmed up
With smudged up make-up
Stumble down the stairs
For a cup of coffee
To get rid of delusion of last night
As you open the door to Jack Frost's smile
You wish you were as snug as a bug in bed
The smell of baker's food is not edible until lunchtime
The day has begun
As customer Mr Impatient begins the daily routine
Of shouting and demanding
It's time to make a perfect smile
And start apologising
As it's drilled into you
Like a screw into wood
The customer's always right, after all
I'm young and under paid
The job's just not worth the £3.50 an hour
My time could be better spent elsewhere.

Kirsty Thomson & Emma Coleman (16)
Kelso High School, Kelso

Rainbow

The colours twinkle high in the sky
As the birds, the bees and the clouds pass by
The rainbow seems to be ever lasting
Curving over and forever glistening
Everyone is searching for that pot of gold
Just waiting at the end, or so the story is told
Red, orange, yellow, blue, indigo, violet and green
A spectacular blend of colours just crying out to be seen
So don't look away for too long

In ten minutes time it will all be gone.

Emily Jones (13)
Kelso High School, Kelso

Seasons

The sun shone in-between the newly grown leaves
Daffodils reaching up to the sky
Tulips opening up slowly
The wind gently pulling and pushing the oak branches
The great oak as tall as a giant
Night and day came and went
The sun getting higher in the sky
Sunflowers start to grow

Spring has come and spring has gone
Sunflowers, now six-foot high tower in the breeze
Heatwaves are everywhere
Daffodils start to die -
Tulips too
Sun is tanning the skin of people
The sun starts to get lower in the sky

Summer has come and summer has gone
The newly grown leaves are now dead
And fall to the ground
Red and brown and yellow are their newfound colours
It rains heavily
Flooding land
It is colder than before

Autumn has come and autumn has gone
The rain is turning into snow
Children play with the snow
Their laughter fills the air
Winter is coming
Winter is here.

Fionn Page (12)
Kelso High School, Kelso

Horse Riding

Thud, thud, thud as I canter round the school
Suddenly I'm coming up to a jump
I'm there and I jump, wee!

I can see everyone watching me
My Highland and I are coming to the next jump
Here it comes
Up and over
Perfect

My pony's called Donald
I can hear everyone cheering it
It's time for my canter
And I'm off
I'm sitting into the saddle
The saddle is really comfy
We're coming to a jump
I sit up and over we go
Perfect, again

It's time to stop
I give Donald a big pat
His soft hairs run through my fingers
He is the best pony ever

I untack him
Leave his tack in the tack room
I brush him
He loves getting brushed
His coat is very shiny

I clean his tack
Take him to his lovely fresh green field for the night.

Daniella Pannone (12)
Kelso High School, Kelso

The Sea

Looking at the sea
A beautiful calm sea
The sun glistening on the surface
Little kids paddling
Shapes of boats bobbing up and down
A nice blue gaze
Hearing people laughing and having a good time

'Oh no! A storm!'
Small waves becoming huge waves
Waves smashing and crashing onto the rocks
People screaming and panicking
Waves lashing out at surfers
Shapes of boats disappearing
Waves rapidly getting bigger, heading to shore
Lightning shooting out of the sky -
'Hold on!'

The dark clouds are clearing
The sun pops out
All that was left was the destruction the sea has done.

Kieran Cook (12)
Kelso High School, Kelso

Winter's Glare

The sun shimmers joyfully on the frozen hills
Making its first appearance to the land of snow

A smile frozen on everyone's faces
As the snow gently falls to the ground like feathers

A layer of snow covers the hilly landscape like icing
As the cold and fresh air spins round the hills like driftwood

As the moon wakes up to the world, so bare
The sun gets a rest from winter's frosty glare.

Joni Falla (11)
Kelso High School, Kelso

Christmas Time Already

It's Christmas time already
And everyone's arrived
My stocking's full to the rim
I hear all the noises of wrapping
I hear all the joys of toys
My cousin Craig has a dinosaur
My sister Claire has a doll
I smell the turkey cooking
Oh! What a wonderful smell
I see all the decorations
The greens, the reds and the whites
I watch all the children playing
I watch all the adults laugh
I taste all the wonderful puddings
I taste all the wonderful food
I have the most wonderful feeling
This Christmas is going to be a:

Blast!

Megan Cuthers (12)
Kelso High School, Kelso

Autumn To Winter

Autumn's passing and winter's coming
The leaves are falling and the trees are bare
The wind is tougher which makes it colder
The time has changed and dark is falling
The morning is lighter and makes it nicer
Christmas is coming so laughter begins
Santa is getting ready for all the young kids
Christmas has passed and that's the end.

Lisa Watson (13)
Kelso High School, Kelso

Bonfire Night

It's dark tonight, you can see the stars
Someone's let off a firework it hasn't exploded
He's going back to light it again
It goes off
Hits him in the face
He's taken to hospital
His family go with him
Everyone else stays to see the rest

The fire smells horrible
People are throwing things on it
They shouldn't be doing that
Boys are getting bored
They start fighting
They're going too near the fire
Phew, they've rolled away
The fireworks are amazing
They're so bright
I like the rockets best
Wait!
Someone's been burnt by a sparkler
He's only five

That's just another Bonfire Night in our street though
It's nothing new
It's the same every year.

Amy Dodds (12)
Kelso High School, Kelso

Hallowe'en

Bang! Crash! Wham! There goes another firework
Lighting up the sky with blues and greens and reds
There's a group of witches coming this way
With scary but sparkly costumes
They have green spotty faces and huge hats

The stars have gone
The sky has gone dull
I can't see much anymore
Now all I can hear is the gentle pitter-patter of raindrops
Wait! *Bang!*
There goes another firework this time the sky's purple and pink

I have a spooky feeling all around me
Like I'm being watched
I turn around
But nobody's there
Now I'm really scared
The rain's gotten heavier
It's crashing down on me now
I wonder where to go, what to do

I feel so alone on this
Spooky, scary night
Now I can see some
Ghosts
They float along in
White sheets -
They're coming towards me
Making ghostly noises
I scream, I no longer like
Hallowe'en.

Melanie King (11)
Kelso High School, Kelso

The Night Walker

As the sun falls
He comes out with his
Long, black shredded up
Coat, which stinks
He drags himself out of
The manhole he calls home
He rakes the streets for food
But as always there is none
So he resorts to killing people
He hides on the roofs and when
He sees a victim he pounces
On them like a tiger, ripping through their flesh

All night he roams the streets
Seeking food, but as the moon
Falls and the sun sets off he
Goes and dives to bed until
Another night rises again.

Sean Robson (14)
Kelso High School, Kelso

Help Me!

There I was just standing there
Nothing to do but to stare
I saw the grenades exploding everywhere
Was it over or had it just begun?

All my friends were now away
I was so lonely out there
So frightened now I know I have to escape

I jumped up and tried to move along
But there was so much going on!
I shouted, I yelled, but nobody heard!

I turned to find that I was going to die
Under the capture of the other side!

Rachael O'Rourke (13)
Kirkintilloch High School, Kirkintilloch

Aftermath

He stands in the wind, silent in dismay
Knows there's no chance, but he can't help but pray
That the others made it out of a dismal, bloody grave
Entirely taken out by the first, murderous wave.

He scans among the dead, looking for familiar faces
Swords and shields scattered around with clubs and brutal maces
He sees a figure far off in the mist
Running towards him with an up-raised fist

He panics, and trips over a spear
Then curls into a ball in his desperate and utter fear
He waits a moment and raises an apprehensive head
There lays his attacker, impaled with a pike and dead

Then he spies a weary man, making not a sound
Then his legs buckle and he crumples to the ground
He rushes over to his saviour's aid who whispers in his ear,
'Get away, hurry now, before more horrors happen here.'

Jack Butler (12)
Kirkintilloch High School, Kirkintilloch

The Accident

Squeak, bash was the only think you could hear
I could not help but turn and stare
The boy is lying very near
Now more people can't help but turn and stare

The wind is blowing by
An ambulance came rushing by
Screams and gasps are all around
The driver beside the boy on the ground
Now the whole street is here
They can't help but turn and stare

The boy's away to the hospital now
I wonder if he'll die
Everyone can't help themselves but turn away and cry.

Katrina Hope (13)
Kirkintilloch High School, Kirkintilloch

Hunter

He thrusts a gnarled claw into the ground
With the light illuminating his eyes
Which burn like fire
Staring around he opens his mouth
A loud, booming growl escaping his throat
His handsome coat fails to be camouflaged
By the surrounding wasteland

A creature passes innocently by
Invading his deadly territory
He lunges forward and sinks in his teeth
Tasting its bitter flesh

But then, his eyes form large circles
He backs away in fear
But with no way out
No way of escaping
He must await his fate

A bang announces the stranger's presence
And with a rustle of leaves it enters
Its teeth are bared in a menacing snare
Gleaming, it looks hungry for revenge

He sprints, but does not seem to move
Frozen to the spot in immense fear
The stranger yells and plunges on top
And snarling it aims for his throat
He wriggles, trying to growl a warning
But his effort is to no avail

A sudden loud bang pierces the air
And he collapses on the ground, blood pouring
Sinking into an eternal sleep
From which he will never wake.

Emma Kinney (12)
Kirkintilloch High School, Kirkintilloch

Peace On Earth

Death and destruction
Everywhere I look
Peace on Earth
What's it worth?
It's just like a game
But no one plays by the rule book
Who will help?
Does anyone else care?

Children cry
Tears fall from their eyes
Peace on Earth
What's it worth?
Families torn apart
By murderers and killers
What's the point
What do people gain?

Bloodshed, dying
Everywhere you turn
Peace on Earth
What's it worth?
Lives are lost
And though we try to forget
They are gone
Never to return

The war is over now
Or is it just beginning?
There's still no peace on Earth
So tell me
What's life worth?

Kim-Michal Blythe (13)
Kirkintilloch High School, Kirkintilloch

The Life Of A Flower

It starts off small
Put into the soil
Hoping that one day
It will be found

Slowly it grows
While being watered and fed
Then one day its head pops up from the ground

As it slowly grows
A bud appears slowly getting bigger
Then just like magic
A flower appears

Day by day it grows and matures
Attracting lots of creatures
All throughout the year

Then winter comes
The flower begins to shrivel up
And eventually dies
At that point it realises
It won't be found again.

Laura Wylie (13)
Kirkintilloch High School, Kirkintilloch

A Snowman's Tale

I started my life as nothing at all
The tiniest snowflake God let fall
Shafts of moonlight through a cloudy sky
Direct my path to where I will lie

Thousands like me, fall to the ground
Nothing around, no noise, no sound
And as dawn breaks in morning light
I'm one of many in a sea of white

The calm is broken by a red gloved hand
As it rolls me across a snow-covered land
Gathering pace we become bigger and bigger
Together we form a strange white figure

Two odd shaped stones become the windows of my soul
As arms thrust through my body, is a wooden pole
And what's that orange thing pushed in my face?
Or those things in my mouth with a horrible taste?

Hour by hour my strength starts to fail
Minute by minute nears the end of my tale
Second by second I trickle and fall
And once again I am nothing at all.

Jonathan Fitzpatrick (12)
Kirkintilloch High School, Kirkintilloch

Christmas Day

The days are getting colder
It's reached that time of year
It's now the month of December
Christmas is coming near

The shops are all buzzing
And full of Christmas glow
Weathermen predicted . . .
A very good chance of snow

Children all excited
Parents are harassed
Credit cards at limits
As money runs out fast

Snow starts falling from the sky
And lying on the ground
Children building snowmen
There's excitement all around

Putting up the decorations
A fairy on the tree
Tinsel twinkling in the light
Christmas colours are all I can see

Finally the waiting is over
And everyone shouts, 'Hooray!'
That is what it's been about
Now it's Christmas Day!

Taylor Kindred (13)
Kirkintilloch High School, Kirkintilloch

The Day That Shocked The World

9/11 that terrible day
4 planes, 3 buildings
They all went up in flames

8 Arabian terrorists
Hijacking the plane
Taking the lives of innocent people

The people, their families
Crying, yelling, screaming
The police were everywhere

Nee-naw, nee-naw
Was all that you could hear
I watched in horror at the incident
And smoke was coming near

'Help, help!' People were screaming
A deserted street with smoke and dirt
2 fallen towers, one half of a pentagon
Now I am getting worried

Tragedy and pain
In all we can say
The burning wreckage
And all the flames

So here I am
A lucky soul
I want to know
Why they would do such a thing?

Greg Halkett (13)
Kirkintilloch High School, Kirkintilloch

Forgiven

As I stand here on this cliff
And I give a final sniff
My tormentors looking snide
The bottom has its arms open wide

As I get ready to jump
And my heart starts to thump
As I leap, I close my eyes
And then open them with surprise

I'm lying on a hill of grass
Not shattered like a pane of glass
I look round and round to see
And wonder, what's happened to me

I see bright gates of gold
Glittering bright and shining bold
I know I have reached Heaven
And I know I've been forgiven.

Thomas Cadden (13)
Kirkintilloch High School, Kirkintilloch

Trapped

Trapped, trapped can't get out
So messed up, just wanna shout

Got to get out, there must be a way
Got to get out or I'll pay

Hour after hour I still search
Knowing they're watching from the perch

Suddenly they swoop and get my hair
Now my hair's been cut my head looks so bare

When the barber cut my hair he said
It was a mat
Now the barber's cut my hair
I'll hit him with a bat.

Alexander Lamb (13)
Kirkintilloch High School, Kirkintilloch

They Always Seem To Find Me

I try not to annoy them
I stay out of their way
But somehow they always seem to find me

I hide in the library
And round the back of the sheds
But somehow they always seem to find me

They kick and punch me
And tell me no one likes me
But the worst part is
I know it's all true

I've told the teachers
But they don't believe me
They say I'm just seeking attention

That made it worse
And now I'm in hospital
They don't know where I am
But somehow they always seem to find me.

Elaine Wright (12)
Kirkintilloch High School, Kirkintilloch

The Burglar

He creeps about at night
I saw him down the stairs
He was eyeing up the biscuit tin
With a hypnotic little glare

He was like a fighter plane
As speedy as can be
He came out empty-handed
He isn't fooling me

'What are you doing in my house?'
'But Son it's only me.'
I never even saw Dad
Standing with a cup of tea.

Gordon Manson (12)
Kirkintilloch High School, Kirkintilloch

Friends Forever

Our friendship is special
Our friendship is true
You are always there for me
And I'll always be there for you

You may feel that you're alone
But no matter what I'm here
When you feel the world's out to get you
Just remember I'll be near

Even when we're far apart
I know I'll be close to your heart
And even when we fight and scream
It is never as bad as it may seem

Because we always make up in the end
Just remember
I'll always be your friend!

Debra Campbell (12)
Kirkintilloch High School, Kirkintilloch

All Alone

Walking alone in the rain
And to keep myself sane
I run lists through my head
Of things to do

Go in, walk the dog
Clean the house, pray to God
That soon someone will come home
To stop me being alone

The afternoon phone call I wait for
To stop me worrying so much
Always waiting by the phone
To stop me being alone.

Ailie McGinley (13)
Kirkintilloch High School, Kirkintilloch

Fear

Fear is the mind killer
All twisted up and strange
Like a sadistic lie spiller
Horrifying and deranged

I imagine a big black hole
Screaming inside out
Driving us almost crazy
Making me want to shout

Like paranoia striking a witness
Of a terrible crime
Like being curled up in a corner
For an entire lifetime

An illusion of perfection
Shattered like a pane of glass
This is the fear you always feel
When it hits you in a mass

There are many fears of things
Sometimes they can be bad
Like sadness of losing a loved one
Feels like you never had

Fear can take your life away
And eat away at your heart
Maybe it's like you're dying inside
A bloodbath or an art . . .

Whatever the explanation
We will never know
It's like an exclamation
That makes you feel so low

Whatever the explanation
Do you really care?
You always feel fear sometime
It's like it's always there.

Callum McClune (13)
Kirkintilloch High School, Kirkintilloch

The Crash

Shattered glass lay everywhere
Wreckage on the road
All the terror
All the pain
Why do people play this game?

Whilst I pass and see them
Lying there
I cannot help but stand and stare
Another life has been taken
Maybe life has been mistaken

Just like that they were gone
Now we're approaching dawn
Why was the road so dark
With faces ghostly white?
We'll never know who's wrong or right!

Paula McLean (13)
Kirkintilloch High School, Kirkintilloch

At Night

The light has been and gone
Now it's darkness all around
There is no light
As it's night

There is a little light from the moon
I know there will be light soon
At night you dream
It's not always what it seems

You're happy when you're asleep
As your emotions run deep
At night you see the stars
At night it might be like Mars

So empty and dark
There is never anybody in the parks.

Lorri O'Neill (12)
Kirkintilloch High School, Kirkintilloch

The Magnificent Game

They call it the magnificent game
They think it is the best
Better than rugby, tennis or cricket
Better than all the rest

Football teams from all over the world
Compete in their cup to win
They come out from the tunnel
Ready to begin

Goals, goals, goals!
It's the best part of the game
The scoring team love to see them
The other thinks they are lame

I like the Scotland international team
With Fletcher, Miller and Pressley
They may not be very good right now
But soon it will be their day

They call it the magnificent game
They think it is the best
Better than rugby, tennis or cricket
Better than all the rest.

Ross Crawford (12)
Kirkintilloch High School, Kirkintilloch

The Hamster And The Dog

Thought he was doing great, my hamster was
Acting like a spy
Climbing up his cage he was
Thinking he could fly

In shock my dog was
So shocked he couldn't stare
Turned and walked, my dog did
And headed for the stair

Hanging on, my hamster was
Kicking in the air
Swinging back and forward
Trying to say it wasn't fair

Splat! My hamster fell
Crack! He hit his head
He simply gave himself a shake
And then he went to bed.

Scott Lang (13)
Kirkintilloch High School, Kirkintilloch

Football

He's just received the ball
And is making a huge run
Taking it by everyone
Having a bit of fun

Listening to the fans
Makes you feel really good
Watch their team score lots of goals
Just the way they should

He took the man to ground
That's worth a yellow card
'I didn't mean to, ref
To go in that hard.'

He takes one last shot at goal
And hits the middle of the bar
A striker comes in for a rebound
But sees it go wide and far.

Andrew Curren (13)
Kirkintilloch High School, Kirkintilloch

Unfallen Tears

I walk along this empty road
The wind picking up fallen leaves
And gently blows my hair off my face
As my home I shall leave

A pressure wells up behind my eyes
And my vision starts to blur
Then I feel a trickle of tears fall down my cheek
And I realise I'm beginning to cry

I wipe them away and take a deep breath
I don't want to let your words get to me
I am stronger than that
Or at least I hope

I don't want you to see
Without you I'm so weak
I want you to think that I am over you
So maybe one day, I will be

But a part of me
Wants you to know the pain you've caused me
By looking in my eyes
With unfallen tears you'll see.

Rebecca McCrosson (13)
Kirkintilloch High School, Kirkintilloch

World War One

I can't stand the groans
Every person has a different moan
Bullets fly past me
They are so close

Every week or so I hear the call
Going over the top in 3, 2, 1
I hate it when they say, 'Stay in line.'
That means we're in range

They can see me
I can't see them
As men fall I hope not me next
I'm not scared of dying

Not seeing my family
Is worst of all
Not getting a 'Hi' when I come home
Not getting to eat home-made soup

As I lie here
I think of them
Never to touch or see them again
I've done it for them.

Iain Taylor (12)
Kirkintilloch High School, Kirkintilloch

Mates

I have a laugh with the boys
Just the three of us
But when they talk about the girls
I can't be bothered with the fuss

We all like the same things
Me and all the guys
CDs, clothes and magazines
That's what we always buy

Our favourite things are fast cars
All of us lads like them
Mercs, Beamers and Lambos
The wheels are full of gems

We're taking our exams early
All my mates and I
When we leave our high school
We're gonna reach up and touch the sky!

Conor Christie (13)
Kirkintilloch High School, Kirkintilloch

Christmas Time

Christmas is getting nearer
Darkness falling at four
Christmas tree coming out
Holly wreath on the door

Shooting stars through the sky
Christmas lights shining bright
Now turkey's being bought
Santa coming out at night

Santa's elves are making toys
Rudolph pulling Santa's sleigh
Santa getting on his suit
Rudolph's nose guiding the way

Stockings above the fire
Presents under the tree
Waking up on Christmas Day
Is the best experience there can be.

Deborah-Ann McLean (13)
Kirkintilloch High School, Kirkintilloch

Anger

Every day I see him
I just want to punch him
Kick him, boot him

He laughs at me
Makes fun of me
Anything to embarrass me

One day when he made fun of me
I shouted, 'Back off!'
He did exactly the opposite

Instead of backing off
He lunged at me
And landed right on top of me

It was so painful
So humiliating
I never wanted to show my face again

I moved schools
Which was good
Because no more bullying for me.

David McCallum (12)
Kirkintilloch High School, Kirkintilloch

Anger

There's a bull inside me, ready to charge
You'll see my anger on your face
It's flowing through my veins, into my heart
The hurt, the pain, the chase

You'll see my anger on your face
I want to make someone feel my pain
The hurt, the pain, the chase
I'll come at you like a downpour of rain

I want to make someone feel my pain
There's a feeling inside me that wants to break free
I'll come at you like a downpour of rain
My anger is looking for the key

There's a feeling inside me that wants to break free
I'll beat you until you're black and blue
My anger is looking for the key
I'll beat you to a pulp, oh how true

I'll beat you until you're black and blue
It's flowing through my veins into my heart
I'll beat you to a pulp, oh how true
There's a bull inside me ready to charge.

Louise Crichton (13)
Loudoun Academy, Galston

Wasted

She sits and she cries
For she is dying inside

She looks out the window at the moon
And she is wondering why . . . no one cares
Do they even know she's there?
And she imagines she's flying to the stars
Because there she can be herself and walk a thousand miles
And she'd never have any sorrows again

She is staring at the wall, nowhere to go
She says that if she could, she'd get to Hollywood
But she hasn't been to her drama lesson in months

Her mam left a year ago, her father's still a drunk
And this girl was just left in-between
When she gets home, Father will beat her
She lies and weeps into the blood, running down her face

She wishes she would die, this depression is so soul-destroying
She's in a deep, dark hole and she can't get out
Her father beats her, her mother left her, her brother tries to help her
But no one can, she thinks no one can, she feels no one can

She screams out loud, shoving her way through piles of unpaid bills,
                                                    out the house door
And runs across her road
No one knows what happened next
But tomorrow, someone will find her lying dead

The suicide may have been painless, the pills, yes they were quick
If only someone had reached out to her
She could have lived, to see her father locked away
Would have seen herself get to the top at Hollywood
But it was wasted, all wasted, her life was wasted.

Rhona Hamilton (13)
Loudoun Academy, Galston

Shark Attack

It was coming
Huge, black eyes
Staring at me, just at me
Coming straight towards me
Faster, faster
Growing huge, filling my vision
Jaws gaping wide
Deep triangular teeth
Made for ripping flesh
It was coming, at me!
Then it flashed deep in my mind
Hit it hard, hard on the nose
I slammed my fist
The pain jarring up my arm
My shoulder wrenched
Pure agony, pure agony
And then it was gone, gone like a flash
Past me, away into the blue
Time stood still
Then I sensed it
Something was there
Dare I turn, dare I look? I had to
I turned around, not wanting to know
Relief flooded over me
Friendly faces gazed upon me
My dive team had come to join me
We surfaced together
Never will I forget that day
The day I survived an attack
Of a great white shark.

Andrew Redmayne (13)
Loudoun Academy, Galston

Hallowe'en

Watch out for witches and bats
While going round houses for sweets
Worst of all spooky black cats
When you go out for trick or treat

While going round houses for sweets
Ghosts and ghouls come out at night
When you go out for trick or treat
Beware, you may get a fright

Ghosts and ghouls come out at night
The wolves all howl at the full moon
Beware, you may get a fright
Hallowe'en will be coming soon

The wolves all howl at the full moon
Worst of all spooky black cats
Hallowe'en will be coming soon
Watch out for witches and bats.

Lindsay Nimmo (13)
Loudoun Academy, Galston

Anger

The anger it wells up inside me
I try to hold it back as long as I can
But all it wants to do is break free
I hold the beast back as long as I can

I try to hold it back as long as I can
They annoy and they poke and provoke
I hold the beast back as long as I can
But when it comes they'll see it's no joke

They annoy and they poke and provoke
It's as black as death on the still, cold night
But when it comes they'll see it's no joke
I see no colours, just blinding light

It's as black as death and the still, cold night
But all I want to do is break free
I see no colours, just blinding light
The anger it wells up inside me.

Robert Young (13)
Loudoun Academy, Galston

Hallowe'en Night

Slimy ghouls
Vicious vampires
Howling werewolves
In the sewers of London town
The lights flicker in the cold, dark houses
The hungry and the rich shake in their beds

As the bloodthirsty zombies grab and scrape their way to the surface
The witches in the caves cackle and fly on their broomsticks
The mouldy mummies slowly walk to the bright lights of London town
The swamp monsters rise from their marshy homes
The ghosts fly through the walls of the Tower of London
And the pumpkin head gallops through the streets with his
                              orange head laughing and shrieking in delight

The frightened children gaze upon the madness outside
                                        from their beds
Wishing that their fun was theirs as well
Because when the sun hits over the horizon
The once scary ghouls will be gone again
Because last night was Hallowe'en night.

Jenni Smith (12)
Loudoun Academy, Galston

Poverty

All alone, cold, wet and hungry
The night draws in and I am illuminated
By the lamp post I sleep
All alone, cold, wet and hungry

All day I work
Under the loom today a boy died
Because of the workman's belt, I can't make a peep
All day I work

I have no money to spare
£500 is what the government funded
A rowdy street with a stalking creep
I have no money to spare

A harvest has come and gone
Another harvest failed
No food for my family to eat
A harvest has come and gone.

Douglas Borland (13)
Loudoun Academy, Galston

My Brother

Michael is my brother
He runs like a horse
He jumps like a kangaroo
He thinks like a computer
He looks like an owl peering into the darkness
He plays basketball like a professional
He jumps like a creature with wings
He speaks like a train rattling past
But when we're alone he's just my brother!

Kelvin Wong (14)
Merchiston Castle School, Edinburgh

The Four Seasons

The cold wind rattles at the windows
The hail hammers against the wall
The snow floats lightly down
This is winter

The buds are opening into flowers
The leaves are growing back on the trees
The days are getting longer
This is spring

The sun beats down on the verdant landscape
The bees buzz happily along
It is as hot as a dragon's breath
This is summer

The leaves fall onto the path
They adorn the pavement
Like a blanket of crisp colours
This is autumn.

Duncan Scott (12)
Merchiston Castle School, Edinburgh

Daydreaming

The sunny, hot beach
As far as the eye can reach
The house by the pool
The wind so inviting and cool
The clouds, soft in the sky
A red sunset is nigh
The golden, sun stroked sand
Fills the beautiful barren waste land
A cluster of dreams
Unreachable it seems
But the place I like to be
Is home, so who needs them? Not me.

Ruaraidh Rafferty (12)
Merchiston Castle School, Edinburgh

Anger

Anger is an army
Waiting to charge
Anger is rubbish
Drifting on a barge

Anger is the smell
Floating through the drains
Anger is the wrath
That's popping out our veins

Anger is a fish
Swimming happily
Waiting for its chance
To take over the sea

Anger is wrong
And never right
So whatever you do
Don't let it take flight.

Joe Sharpe (11)
Merchiston Castle School, Edinburgh

Up In The Air

When I was at 10,000 feet
I was gliding like a bird
I was the greatest flyer in the world
But I was not scared, but then
Bang
The engine blew
Bang then again
I was going down
Further, further going down
But I did not struggle
For I knew what was the point?
I just let myself go and down, down I went.

David Barclay (13)
Merchiston Castle School, Edinburgh

The Moment

The sky was a cloudless blue
We drove ever inwards towards the Spanish countryside
It was a rolling green land full of heavy olive trees
Under their shade we stopped for a picnic
As I sat down my eyes fixed on the thick, lush grass
In its midst there was a movement
A twitch
It was then that I saw it was a snake
Squirming like a hose under pressure
It coiled and rolled
It rippled and squirmed
For me it was a play thing
I took to my feet and grabbed the nearest stick
I hit and struck the writhing thing
The movement stopped
Its head rose like a periscope
It lunged and bit me
Hard on the finger
I held my injury up and cried
A trophy I would never forget.

Guillermo Ruiz Alvarez (12)
Merchiston Castle School, Edinburgh

Poem

I have so much hate
I can't control my fate
I am a speck in the sky
A needle in a haystack
I am so full of anticipation -
I can't tell what is going to happen
It is like a swarm of bees round a
Honey pot and I am the honey
There is nothing I can do but wait
For my fate.

Christopher Grieve (13)
Merchiston Castle School, Edinburgh

Honour And Fear

Here I am with my wings extended from side to side like the
blades of the windmills

I feel I am privileged, but can that privilege be worth my life?
I remember my house back in the village with all the people
and their wives
Mine should be waiting for a man that will never return
For that I am sorry, but in Heaven or Hell we shall have
a meeting again

The bullets go from west to east, from north to south
Like beasts they shall have a feast on the cold metal of my
flying bird's rear

My airplane has been hit
Should I flee and surrender to fear or should I stay for the honour
even if it's only a bit?

My decision is made, I shall stay and for my wife's honour
I shall be slayed

Although my time has come I hope she finds another love
Because in the afterlife we are sure to meet again.

Jose Rodriguez (14)
Merchiston Castle School, Edinburgh

Need

I see all the people playing
Some of them with their friends
Some of them with their family
And I'm here, alone, writing this poem
That seems to me as a story
I need my country to tell the story
I need my friends to just laugh again
I need my family to stop crying
A bed to fall asleep
I just need my mom to wake me up again.

Roberto de Zatarain Rugarcia (14)
Merchiston Castle School, Edinburgh

The Rock

I was walking
High and low
Far and wide
Landscapes changing from minute to minute

Then I came upon a beautiful scene
Water falling great heights and landing
In a pool
As clear as sparkling crystal

I waded
Into the shallows
Walking amongst rocks and flowers

Then it caught my eye
This perfect rock
As white and as smooth as an eye
Within a spider web of ice blue colours

A perfect stone
All curves and lines
A stone to cherish.

Duncan Nicholls (13)
Merchiston Castle School, Edinburgh

Tranquillity Or Not!

Flying high
700,000 feet above sea level
Once a peaceful wilderness high above the sky
Now polluted with gasses, planes and gunshots reflecting off
each other
Beneath me, a puddle of blood and rotting human carcasses
It's the only way forward or so they tell me
What do they know?
Controlling me from beneath
Who do they think they are, telling us we have to fly to the skies
leaving our beloved families behind us?

Cameron Shaw (13)
Merchiston Castle School, Edinburgh

Poem Of Soul Feeling

You are my soul
My life and its reason
I think of you
As the four seasons

Spring for the growth
Of the plants and the flowers
Summer for the beautiful sun
Staying out for hours

Autumn for the cool breeze
While walking in a field
And winter for the icy snow
And you, my blazing fire as my shield

I never want those feelings
To leave me behind
Freezing to death
With no one to find.

Fergus Robson (13)
Merchiston Castle School, Edinburgh

Auntie Elma

I've got an auntie Elma who has bristles on her tongue
Just like a cat

After eating a whole pack of Whiskers
She wants to go straight to sleep on our doormat

In the afternoon you would find her all curled up at the bottom of
my bed
Her tail touching the back of her small round head

As you can see my auntie Elma is not of this land
Her feline appearance is what makes her so grand

Her fangs are like needles as menacing as sharp claws
I always have to tell my friends, beware of her paws.

Roman Kermani (12)
Merchiston Castle School, Edinburgh

Fireworks

Boom! Snarl! Crack!
Up, up and away it flew
Into the twinkling sky
The first rocket of Bonfire Night
Laid out on the grass
Full of loaded explosion
Were twisters, bangers, rockets and whistlers
All were waiting to explode with energy

A second rocket went off
Wheeee!
Suddenly there was a cascade of yellow, green, blue and red
All the colours glittered and faded
Shimmered and shattered
Glittering and falling
Dying in the night sky.

Andrew Spears (12)
Merchiston Castle School, Edinburgh

The Tree Climber

I'm a boy who likes to climb trees
One day I climbed this old fossil
Crick, crick! Crick, crick! Went the giant grasshoppers
The bark on the tree was as rough as hairy leather
Higher and higher I climbed until
I could touch the big blue Tanzanian sky
I stepped onto a long thin branch
Crack! And down, down plunged I to the ground
Crash! I landed on a heap of branches
I looked at my hand and saw that it was as limp as a piece of cloth
Then I felt the pain, a knife in my heart
I waited for what seemed like an age
Then I saw my brother's face and heard
The sound of rescue approaching.

Andrew Boyd (12)
Merchiston Castle School, Edinburgh

The Bully

The clock had struck ten and
The screams of
Children filled the corridors
Running through this corridor and that
Corridor
They reached the playground
There stood
The dreaded bully
The sun was beating down
The bully grabbing this child and that
Child
He would guard his territory like a lion
I needed to get to the
Other exit
But I couldn't
My lunch money was slipping away
I ran, I ran as fast as I
Could, but he had me like a lion catching
Antelope for lunch
My money spilling like hard rain
He retrieved his award and threw
Me into the corner
For the beating.

Michael Nicol (12)
Merchiston Castle School, Edinburgh

Autumn

A utumn is the time when the leaves turn brown and fall off the trees
U nder the trees the squirrels gather acorns
T he birds fly south for the warmer weather
U p above the weather starts to get cold
M ountains become inaccessible
N ight falls and all the animals wait for winter.

Rory McMenigall (11)
Merchiston Castle School, Edinburgh

Christmas Morning

(But not as we know it)

His hands were cold and frail
Shiny and slimy
His voice was like a frog croaking
I was unable to move from his snake-like stare
He also had a grip like a shark
His teeth were sharp and shiny
He scrambled up and started to walk like a chicken
He was opening my presents, laughing as he went
Mum shouted
He shouted back
They both fought throwing words like stones
Mum walked off
Uncle walked off
Another Christmas morning ruined.

Harry Clark (13)
Merchiston Castle School, Edinburgh

My Father

My father, as tall as a redwood
With a voice as loud as an elephant's cry
And muscles as strong as a boxer

He lacks in nothing
He is more skilful than Michael Jordan
And as smart as Albert Einstein

The only offence I have against him
The one thing he lacks
Is the hair on his head

But if I open my mouth
And spit it all out
I am left face first on the floor.

David Black (12)
Merchiston Castle School, Edinburgh

My First Memorable Autumn

Many colours
Autumn day
Many people
Every day

Colder, colder

The dark blue evening sky
Drifting
Drifting into winter

Colder, colder

Fighting for the conkers
Leaves have fallen
Many colours

Colder, colder

Birds are going westward
Westward

Hedgehogs burrowing deep
Deep

To save themselves from

The death of summer.

Matthew Gorrie (13)
Merchiston Castle School, Edinburgh

Past Poem

I sat on the floor on a summer's day
It was warm and the sun was shining as it was Saturday
I rested my feet gently on a bundle of hay, the sun's orb rose
Up and I couldn't help but say, 'What a beautiful day.'

I looked to the north
There it rested
A beautiful bird with a big red chest
This was the best
A place where I could finally rest

I could hear the butterfly's wings
Chattering in the wind
Like a pack of hyenas.

Jamie Stewart (14)
Merchiston Castle School, Edinburgh

The School Run

The drive, the long, long drive
Seems endless on the school run
'Pack your bags!' shouts Dad up the stairwell
We rush, hearts pounding
To make it on time
Squashed and cornered by the bags
Our home grows smaller and smaller
My only good thought
Is that at least I'll be taller
On my return.

Alex Ruff (13)
Merchiston Castle School, Edinburgh

Flying Through The Sky

I'm flying through the sky
Through the immense and
Blue sky in the middle of the war
The noise of bullets make me the
Happiest man in the world
I enjoy this, this is the best
Thing of my life and this is
Flying through the blue sky

I'm walking on the air
Feeling like a bird on the
Wind, and I think to myself
What is over there? I'm as beautiful
As a mockingbird even when I sing.

Emilio Maurer (14)
Merchiston Castle School, Edinburgh

Ross

His ginger hair is like a neon light
It splits the scene

This glare would frighten a dragon!
His stride covers valleys
But when he smiles he lights up the whole night sky

He could start 10 new world wars

Despite this, he is my brother
When he smiles he's a fire cracker
Of laughter

His jokes would bring the world a smile.

Craig Lumsden (13)
Merchiston Castle School, Edinburgh

Seaside

As I approached the beach
I felt a twist of nerves in my stomach
Before me were waves as big as a house
Curling and crashing, gnawing and chewing the shore

Slowly I entered knee-deep
I stood in freezing water
The foam frothed and bubbled
My heart pounded like a crazy drum
Despite the tight reassuring hand of my father
Deeper and deeper we waded
The enormity and power all around me engulfed me
I wanted to run, to escape
My father laughed in derision

The wave hit me like a wall
I went tumbling back
I thought I was going to go forever
But a huge strain on my arm told me not
Then it was over
I was lying on the beach, elated
I was safe.

Hugh Bambridge (12)
Merchiston Castle School, Edinburgh

My Mum's A Cookbook

My mum's a cookbook with all kinds of ideas
My mum's as sticky as toffee peaches all warm and soft
My mum's as delicious as a chocolate pudding
My mum's as comforting as hot tomato soup
My mum's as spicy as chicken fajitas
My mum's as fruity as a rich Christmas cake
My mum's as sweet as a strawberry soufflé
My mum's a cookbook with all kinds of ideas.

Ruaraidh Drummond (12)
Merchiston Castle School, Edinburgh

The Enemy

I wondered, high in the sky in my plane,
Thinking of the enemy. You couldn't see
Him anywhere, just a clear beautiful sky
No clouds, no nothing, just a nice shiny sun

Black tiny points appeared in front of me
Moving rapidly through the skies. Closer and
Closer you could feel the fear of getting wounded
Or shot. Bullets came from everywhere, getting
Into other planes and killing people

The enemy, cruel, killing everyone:
Not caring about anything is what makes war
So bloody, sad and upsetting for families and
Such a massacre.

Lazaro Hernandez (14)
Merchiston Castle School, Edinburgh

The Swan

Her soft white feathers
Blow in the breeze
They can stand it in all kinds of weathers
She's so well wrapped up she could never freeze
She's got all sorts of ideas, she's so clever

Her tall, elegant neck
She can see whatever's going on
She can attack you with an almighty peck
You better get running or she'll carry on
She is so beautiful, she is so fine
She is without doubt something divine.

James Gell (11)
Merchiston Castle School, Edinburgh

The Farmyard

As I moved around the dark and frightening farm buildings
The shadows became like twisted figures as wild as tigers
Turning, twisting, trailing in the light breeze
I turned and twirled around in the panic to find a way out
Then I saw it, a ray of light in the building shadows as dark as night
I sprinted, with the figures snapping at my flying heels
The light rained over me like a piece of Heaven thrown down to Earth
I listened to all the noises; the hen was a determined mother teaching
her demanding children
The rapid rats rioted in the morning stillness
A lamb was a toddler calling for its mother into the confusing crowds
of the packed street
I continued my journey on towards the woodland playground I had
set out to find
Leaving the cacophony behind.

Harry Fletcher (13)
Merchiston Castle School, Edinburgh

My Mum's Apple Crumble

My mum's apple crumble is the best in the world
With the custard lapping at the sides

My mum's apple crumble is really good
It has to be my favourite type of food

When I have firsts, I just want seconds
Almost as if the food beckons

My mum's apple crumble is rather unique
With the gooey bit underneath

I don't know what I would do without my mum
But especially her apple crumble.

George Erlanger (11)
Merchiston Castle School, Edinburgh

Summer Farm

His hair was as black as coal
His face was as white as snow
He walked in the door and then flopped onto the floor
He must have been bitter with cold
He stood up and collapsed into a seat
We turned up all of the heat
The following day he awoke with a cold
His nose was as red as a fat clown's nose
His eyes were running like sprinklers
He needed some of the sun's hot rays
He'd be back on the farm in the next few days
Sure enough after a couple of days he was back on the farm
Soaking up the rays.

Dougie Duff (13)
Merchiston Castle School, Edinburgh

Mum And Dad

My dad is a farmer
Big hands, tall man
He smells of oil and cows
You would think that this would stink
But somehow, it is comforting

My mum is a brill cook
Standing over the Aga for ages
Trying to make a new dish
Like her Moroccan lamb
It was yummy.

Angus Lindsay (11)
Merchiston Castle School, Edinburgh

Snow

What is it? I asked
What is snow?
It is so bright
It is so white
Blinding to the eye

What is it? I asked
What is snow?
It just causes trouble
It jams up the roads and
Turns pavements into ice rinks

What is it? I asked
What is snow?
It's frozen rain
It's cold, it's icy and it turns your hands numb

What is it? I asked
What is snow?
It is like a blanket that covers everything on ground
It is so beautiful
But when you touch it it's wet and cold

What is it? I asked
What is snow?
Why is it so cold?
What causes it?
What is snow?

Adam Linton (11)
Merchiston Castle School, Edinburgh

My Little Brother

My little brother
Wee though he may be
He still finds the time
To try and beat me!

He's on the PlayStation
All day and all night
But no matter what win
No matter how many fights

We fight a lot, us two
Oh yes, we do, we do
But in the end we always make up
No more grudges, no more fuss

When he is in bed
I often struggle not to wake him up
Just to annoy him
So the fight starts up again!

In the morning he's a roaring laugh
Until it is time for his early morning bath
He refuses to wash and keep clean
That's why he smells so mean!

As time moves on
I begin to think
He is not as bad
As I often think.

Kyle Smith (13)
Merchiston Castle School, Edinburgh

The Football Match

The car shot along the motorway like a bullet from a gun
The journey was long but the chat was fun

The queue was as long as a giant snake
The tickets were thankfully not fake

The seats were as smooth as a boy's cheek
The singing was as good as a robin's beak

The team was as good as a summer's holiday
The goals were as good as a Christmas holiday

The score was a 3-0 win
We put the other team in the 'sin bin'.

Hamilton McMillan (13)
Merchiston Castle School, Edinburgh

Drugs

Drugs are bad
Drugs make you sad
Injecting things into your body
I can assure you it will make you sorry
Once you have one
The deed is done
You've taken it in
Now you'll end up eating out of bins
Everyone's read
'Drugs make you dead'
They take it, they take it, in till they drop
Now their life is at a stop!

Edward Henderson-Howat (11)
Merchiston Castle School, Edinburgh

The Duck And The Squirrel

There once was a duck that was really out of luck
And he didn't know what to do
Then down came a squirrel from on top of the hill
And said, 'I'll get some luck for you!'

For he was a magic squirrel
From on top of the hill
And he helped the duck
To find some luck
And so his life was fulfilled

They searched high, they searched low, they searched fast, they
searched slow

But they could not find any luck
They searched everywhere, they were in despair
But squirrel said, 'We'll not give up!'

For he was a magic squirrel
From on top of the hill
And he helped the duck
To find some luck
And so his life was fulfilled

They were almost through and they didn't know what to do
Then suddenly by the sea
Squirrel found some luck for his friend duck
Then they both shouted with glee

For he was a magic squirrel
From on top of the hill
And he helped the duck
To find some luck
And so his life was fulfilled.

Tim Balfour (12)
Merchiston Castle School, Edinburgh

What Is Anger?

Anger is like a fiery oven
It bursts like a volcano
It wants to strike and strike
It attacks until it is satisfied
It is like a red-hot fiery ball of flame
Lashing out and burning whatever it touches

People annoying you just make you want to hit out in anger
Your face turns red as a demon with frustration
You just want to stomp off and do the opposite to what you are told
Anger controls you
You can't give anger away
You can't let go of anger
Anger is you
Anger is everyone

When you are angry, you take it out on everyone else
Everything in the world seems wrong, nothing seems right
When you are angry, you scream and shout
Just like a hundred herds of elephants running down the streets
Hitting out at everything as they go

Killing animals for fun makes me angry
Being told off for things you haven't done makes me angry
Hearing about people murdering others for no reason makes me angry

When you are angry, everyone else in the world takes it out on you
Nothing can ever be right when you are angry.

Ben Erlanger (14)
Merchiston Castle School, Edinburgh

The Pizza

The great big Aga is standing tall
The pizza is ready to cook
I slide it onto the pizza paddle . . .
And as it enters the towering oven
I take a breath . . .
Wish it luck . . . then let it go

Those tortuous 28 minutes take forever to pass
I want to look, to see if it's bubbling on the surface
But no, I have to leave it!
At last the timer 'dings'
I race towards the door
It opens with a gush of hot cheesy steam -
The air is filled with spicy pepperoni and mozzarella

And what a glorious sight!
Browned at the edges
Perfect pepperoni
Mozzarella steaming hot
But the final test
The taste!

Mmmm . . . what a taste!
The ingredients are the perfect amount
But then I hear a pleading cry . . .
'Can I have some?'

Angus Paterson (11)
Merchiston Castle School, Edinburgh

Fun In The Sky

I'm so high
I could touch the sky
I'm dancing through the skies
Through gunshot

I laugh at all them beneath
Who aren't here
Cowards, fools, how can
They miss out on all the
Fun?

When hit, you see
Your whole life flashes before you
But there's no shame
For I did my best

Bang! Hitting the ground
Your soul leaves you
Going up to a far
Better place

I laugh at those beneath
Who aren't here
Cowards, fools, how can they miss out on all
The fun?

Marinus Maris (14)
Merchiston Castle School, Edinburgh

Freedom

I am free up here
Higher than the clouds
Silence, just me
But then I go back
I must always go back
It's a lose-lose situation
Don't drop the bombs and get
Sent to the front line
Drop the bombs and risk getting shot
You can never get eternal freedom
Freedom lasts as long as fuel.

Campbell Paton (13)
Merchiston Castle School, Edinburgh

The Terrier

In a flask of brown and black
A terrier runs at high speed
Flies back and then hits a stone wall
Its yap is a penetrating cry
It looks like a brush, it feels like a brush, but brushes don't bite
Teeth like diamonds, hair like bristles
Smashing through vases, biting through wires
It snuffles around digging up plants
Barking at squirrels, chasing them up trees
Annoying big dogs and then cowering away
But what's the fuss?
It's only a puppy.

Rob Dickson (11)
Merchiston Castle School, Edinburgh

Live

I'm here in the house
Near my bed I put my head
Everything is in silence
It's midnight, I'll try to sleep a bit
I look through the window
And I just see all out there
The rain, the grass green
All these leaves that already fell
And I remember my family
I ask myself
What am I going to be doing in 10 or 20 years?
Am I going to see these people again?
Why does God want me to be here?
Why not there with my family and friends?
I don't know all these answers
But I know something else
We have to live our own life, don't envy others
Because life is life
And we are given only one.

Jaime Arroyo (13)
Merchiston Castle School, Edinburgh

Autumn

When grass has grown and October comes
The grass falls down
In October times
The grass, a green carpet in summer
For the children to play
In autumn becomes a multicoloured rug
And the children are gone
Next little flying flakes fall
A white carpet appears
For the children to play.

Vlad Mackenzie (11)
Merchiston Castle School, Edinburgh

My Baby Sister

Holding onto her bear
Continuing to sit and stare
Sitting there on the floor
Someone you have to adore

At night she always screams
Occasionally, thankfully, she has peaceful dreams
When she grows up she will always be
My baby sister
A cherished addition to our family!

Kerr Aitken (13)
Merchiston Castle School, Edinburgh

Ellie

She jumped up high and sat on my lap
Her eyes were moist and brown, pleading
As if she was starving and full of needing

She ate the food while she could
Then sat on my chair like I new she would
She licked my hand and took a bone
Then sneaking off to rest for the night.

Grant Hardie (13)
Merchiston Castle School, Edinburgh

Autumn

Brown and crispy leaves drop from the trees
And Hallowe'en's here
Ready to be thrown aside the leaves lie there
Conkers fall and acorns drop
And little red squirrels come to eat them
Like a herd of horses, boys race
They finish the chase
To pick conkers.

Nathan Kupisz (11)
Merchiston Castle School, Edinburgh

The Drunken Horse

One ice-cold dark night
A drunken father of mine was in a car snorting with zs
My mother was not pleased at all
Driving mile by mile we felt like we had picked up an
                                    unwanted hitchhiker
Home sweet home arrived to our joy the drunken man awoke
He could not stand, his body slumped like an old sack

Warmth captured us and pulled us in, but his face was lost in sleep
Gingerly we lifted him, a dead weight
He struggled to awaken and face the lights
Some time later the horse fell asleep
Inhaling the dust from the carpet floor.

Justin Chu (13)
Merchiston Castle School, Edinburgh

The Magnificent 47

Born in Cardiff a Welsh dragon is he
Faster than a cheetah his name be Bellamy
Coventry to Newcastle the Magpies and Bobby
Hoped he'd stay and become a Geordie

Firing in goals and winning games
Souness arrived and it burst into flames
Celtic offered a chance to come
Bellamy grabbed it and off he run

His first against Clyde he curled one in
From then on he couldn't stop scorin'
Caley, Hibs, the Dons, and United
The winner against Gers and the fans were delighted

The fans and players want you to stay
Forget about the money please don't go away
Barcelona, Milan, next season's a different story
Stay at Celtic and take the glory.

Derek Hudson (14)
Oakbank School, Aberdeen

Bars From Life

These four walls
I can't see anything else at all
Except for one thing
The barred window on the wall

Out there is called life
People hand in hand
I am here and lonely
I'm forever damned

No one looks through it
It's only me
Nothing special here
Nothing good to see

They all have companions
There with their friends
But I'm stuck in here
This until my end.

Andrew Ferguson (16)
Our Lady's High School, Seafar

Rain

I love to walk in the pouring rain as
No one can see my pain the tears I shed
Of anguish and fear, love and hate of my
Sorrows that this world create

I loved to walk in the pouring rain, hand
In hand with my pain, the tears running down my face
People think, that it's just the rain
And pay no attention to this my pain

Kiss me in the pouring rain, to wash away my
Fear and hate, to wash me with love and hope
My sadness drowned in the puddle below.

Jaclyn Mead (15)
Our Lady's High School, Seafar

A Scared Love

Tracing your face with the tip of my finger
I follow your smile, I halt and I linger
I want to stay here, forever in awe
Yet knowing I can't. I so fear that you saw
The look in my eyes
Of love and surprise
The way I so want
The way you so taunt
Without even knowing
It's killing me slowly
Oh, how bad I need
And how you on lead
Me into your trap
I'm falling apart
You've got me; I'm yours
Of shame I am poor
And so here lies my finger
And it still does linger
Yet you do not trace
The path of my face
For my love isn't shared
It's so harsh, and I'm scared.

Laura McLoone (16)
Our Lady's High School, Seafar

Benidorm

Benidorm
Excited
Happy
Went with my friend
Swimming with dolphins
Saw the seals
People talking
It was fun
At the beach
People having fun
Smelt the salty sea
I got burnt
But, I went brown
Went to Water World
Smelt the chlorine
Went to the shows
It was exciting
Went out at night
To the Rainbow Bar
Smelt the beer
Lots of people
Having fun
Coming home
I felt so sad
Wanted to stay longer.

Catherine Watson (13)
Snowdon School, Stirling

At Home

At home
With my mum
Baking
Baking cakes
Sounds like fun

Candles are burning
On the fire place
Music jumping

Plants
Green and red
Water sucking in
Plants growing

Door knocking
Children's laughter
Feel so happy
At home.

Donna Kilpatrick (15)
Snowdon School, Stirling

Outfit From Uncle George

About five
White outfit
All in one
Always wore
Joined together
Purple and white
It's mine
Meant a lot
From Uncle George.

Natasha Todd (14)
Snowdon School, Stirling

My Home Town

My hometown
Peterhead
The place I love
And want to be
Mostly cold
But good to me
I wouldn't change it
If I could
Because that's the place
I long to be
My little niece
Looks up to me
She's little and sweet
And loves being with me
I love her and can't wait
To be free
So I can do things
Just her and me.

Kerry Lee Youngson (15)
Snowdon School, Stirling

Beach

People walking dogs
Breeze on my face
Sea roaring
Rocks clashing
Watching the sea
Taste salt in mouth
Sand sparkling
In the sunlight
Clouds clearing
Sky bright.

Louise Youngson (15)
Snowdon School, Stirling

Blackpool Pleasure Beach

'Tis like a buzz
Your heart races on
The big Pepsi
People screaming
Scared, excited
Blood rushing from head to toe

Blackpool pleasure beach
Shows big and small
Lots of movement
All around
Spinning
Toppling
Tumbling about

Rainbow colours
Strike your eyes
Bright and sparkly
Happy people

Sand and water
Sun shimmers
Children swimming
Loud shouts of laughter
Baby dipping feet

Leaving
Miserable
Gloomy
Exhausted
But happy.

Andrea Raeburn (15)
Snowdon School, Stirling

Fly Away

Where do you start, where do I begin?
It's such a mess that I've got myself in
Head full of thoughts, fears and sorrow
What's gone on today, what will happen tomorrow?

Doubt is a thing always on my mind
Thoughts of the past I try to leave behind
This sort of place, it's not okay
I'd rather be free and fly away

Leave it all for another day
I try to remember it will not always be this way

All the anger and all the pain
Constantly drives me insane
Trying to forget and not look back
Trying to get myself back on track

I've got to sort my head out
And realise what life is about
I'd rather be free and fly away
It doesn't matter what I do or say.

It's the same story everyday
So I think I'd rather fly away
All this pain it cannot last
Soon it will all be in the past

And life will be bright and good
Life will be the way it should
And I won't need to
Fly away.

Lisa Keenan (15)
Snowdon School, Stirling

Edinburgh

Edinburgh
A good town
Amazing

Edinburgh
I love it
Just great

Edinburgh
Difficult times
Sad

Edinburgh
The shopping
Marvellous

Leith
Good shopping
Food and stuff

I like to be in Edinburgh
With my friends.

Charleigh Cairns (14)
Snowdon School, Stirling

Pollock Park

Trees blowing in the wind
Smell of pine in the air
Golfers in the field
Mum, Dad walking
Slowly by my side

Hear the waterfall in the background
Kim and James running ahead

Walk closer to water
Watch - don't fall in
Water dangerous - fast currents
Feeling uneasy near the water

See Kim and James laughing
From the corner of my eye
See squirrel running along
Hear horses on the grass
Clip-clop, clip-clop

Autumn - feeling happy
Kim and James playing tag
On the grass

Animals - all kinds of animals
Love going there
I feel great.

Ashleigh Green (15)
Snowdon School, Stirling